Azad Hind
Writings and Speeches
1941–43

Anthem South Asian Studies
Series Editor: Crispin Bates

Azad Hind
Writings and Speeches
1941–43

SUBHAS CHANDRA BOSE

EDITED BY
SISIR BOSE AND SUGATA BOSE

Anthem Press
London

This edition first published by Anthem Press 2004

Anthem Press is an imprint of
Wimbledon Publishing Company
75-76 Blackfriars Road
London SE1 8HA
or
PO Box 9779, London SW19 7QA

This edition first published in 2002 by Permanent
Black, Delhi, India.

This edition © Netaji Research Bureau 2002
is reprinted by arrangement with the Netaji Research Bureau
and the original publisher and is only for sale outside South Asia.

All rights reserved. No part of this publication may be reproduced, stored in a retrieval system, or transmitted, in any form or by any means, without the prior permission in writing of Wimbledon Publishing Company, or as expressly permitted by law, or under terms agreed with the appropriate reprographics rights organization.

British Library Cataloguing in Publication Data
Data available

Library of Congress in Publication Data

A catalogue record has been applied for
1 3 5 7 9 10 8 6 4 2

ISBN 1 84331 082 1 (Hbk)
ISBN 1 84331 083 X (Pbk)

Typeset by Pentagon Graphics Pvt. Ltd., India
Printed in India

CONTENTS

List of Illustrations	viii
Dr Sisir Kumar Bose and Netaji's Work	ix
Acknowledgements	xii
Introduction	1

Writings and Speeches

1. **A Post-dated Letter**
   To Hari Vishnu Kamath, 18 January 1941 — 11

2. **Forward Bloc: Its Justification**
   The Kabul Thesis, 22 March 1941 — 12

3. **Plan of Indian Revolution**
   Report of an Interview — 32

4. **Secret Memorandum to the German Government**
   Berlin, 9 April 1941 — 36

5. **Supplementary Memorandum to the German Government**
   Berlin, 3 May 1941 — 48

6. **Secret Message to Comrades in India**
   May 1941 — 51

7. **Draft of the Free India Declaration**
   'Mazzotta', May 1941 — 54

8. **A Gloomy Scenario**
   Letter to Dr Woermann of the German Foreign Office, 5 July 1941 — 56

9. **The Russo-German War and Indian Struggle**
   Report of a Conversation with the German Foreign Office, 17 July 1941 — 57

10. **The Approach of an Enemy**
    Letter to German Foreign Minister von Ribbentrop, 15 August 1941 — 59

11. **Address Me as O. Mazzotta**
    Letter to Naomi Vetter, Autumn 1941 — 62

12	The Fall of Singapore First Broadcast, 19 February 1941	63
13	Seize This Opportunity Broadcast, 11 March 1942	65
14	Burmese Freedom Broadcast, 13 March 1942	67
15	India has no Enemy Outside Her Own Frontiers Broadcast, 19 March 1942	71
16	My Death is Perhaps an Instance of Wishful Thinking Broadcast, 25 March 1942	75
17	An Open Letter to Sir Stafford Cripps Broadcast, 31 March 1942	79
18	India for the Indians Broadcast, 6 April 1942	82
19	Compromise-Hunting is Like War-Mongering Broadcast, 13 April 1942	84
20	My Allegiance Broadcast, 1 May 1942	89
21	I Should be in the East Letter to German Foreign Minister von Ribbentrop, 22 May 1942	94
22	Face to Face with the German Führer Record of the Conference between Hitler and Bose, 29 May 1942	96
23	Statement to the World Press June 1942	103
24	The Pledge of the INA Address to the Indian Legion in Europe and Broadcast, June 1942	106
25	Link up Indian Nationalists All Over the World Message to the Bangkok Conference, 15 June 1942	108
26	Differentiate between Internal and External Policy Broadcast, 17 June 1942	110
27	Full Support to Gandhi Early August 1942	115

CONTENTS

28	**The Quit India Movement** Broadcast, 17 August 1942	125
29	**Join India's Epic Struggle** Broadcast, 31 August 1942	132
30	**Free India and Her Problems** August 1942	140
31	**India and Germany** Speech 11 September 1942	149
32	**The USA, Britain and India** Broadcast, 15 October 1942	154
33	**Somewhere Near India** Letter to German Foreign Minister von Ribbentrop, 5 December 1942	162
34	**The Situation in Europe** Broadcast, 7 December 1942	165
35	**The Duty of Patriotic Indians** Broadcast, 1 January 1943	172
36	**Independence Day** Speech, 26 January 1943	174
37	**The Bluff and Bluster Corporation of British Imperialists** Speech, Late January/Early February 1943	184
38	**The 24th Anniversary of the Bloodbath of Amritsar** Speech, End January/Early February 1943	191
39	**On the Path of Danger** Letter to Sarat Chandra Bose, 8 February 1943	195

List of Illustrations

1. Subhas Bose on his arrival in Berlin, April 1941.
2. A page from the Kabul Thesis.
3. Subhas Bose at his desk, working under the cover name 'Orlando Mazzota'.
4. Subhas Bose with the First Officers' Corps of Indian Legion in Europe.
5. A portrait, Berlin, 1942.
6. Subhas Bose at his desk in Berlin, 1942.
7. Subhas Bose speaking at the inauguration of the Indo-German Friendship Society in Hamburg, 1942.
8. In the garden of his house in Berlin.
9. Subhas Bose addressing the Indian Independence Day meeting in Berlin, 26 January 1943.
10. Subhas Bose with Abid Hasan on the submarine.

Dr Sisir Kumar Bose and Netaji's Work[1]

Netaji's charioteer during the great Escape on those two fateful nights of 16 and 17 January 1941 left us all bereft on 30 September 2000. In the second week of December 1940 Netaji had called Sisir Bose to his side and asked him in Bengali: '*Amar ekta kaj korte parbe?*'. From that magical moment Sisir Bose never stopped doing Netaji's work. All morning on 30 September 2000 he was working away in the Chairman's office next to Netaji's bedroom, making certain that the generations to come would continue to learn from Netaji's book of life. On his last visit to the Netaji Research Bureau Netaji's friend Dilip Kumar Roy had said: '*Sisir, janoto loyalty kathatar kono Bangla sathik pratishabda hoyna, karon amra Bangalira loyal hote janina. Tumi kintu loyalty kake bale ta dekhie diyechho.*' (Sisir, there is no exact Bengali equivalent of the word loyalty because we Bengalis do not know how to be loyal. But you have shown what loyalty truly means.')

For the crime of 'assisting Subhas Chandra Bose', Sisir suffered imprisonment in Calcutta's Presidency Jail, Delhi's Red Fort, the Lahore Fort and Lyallpur Jail between 1942 and 1945, the years covered in Volumes 11 and 12 of Netaji's Collected Works. In the post-independence period, alongside his untiring work as one of India's leading pediatricians, he devoted himself to the task of preserving the best traditions of India's freedom movement.

What Dr Sisir Kumar Bose tried to achieve, through the Netaji Research Bureau, to preserve and protect Netaji's historic legacy, is best expressed in a Bengali poem 'Uttaradhikar' that he wrote on his 80th birthday on 2 February 2000:[2]

> This life of ours
> A portrait of fulfilment,
> The task of preserving the inheritance
> was a heavy one indeed.
> But it was achieved,

---

1 Dr Sisir Kumar Bose did not live to see Volumes 11 and 12 of Netaji's Collected Works in print. This is a brief tribute to his lifelong devotion to a cause.

2 Translated by Sumantra Bose.

that's a story unto itself.
Fifty years of struggle,
hand in hand, together,
Recording history, reading politics,
and above all keeping alive the mission
of patriotism, public service.
This life of ours
is blessed
with love, dedication and, service.

In the words of our great poet-philosopher Rabindranath Tagore: '*Shikha theke shikha jwalate hoy. Tanr sei paripurna jeeban theke amader agni grahan korte habe.*' (A flame has to be lit from a flame. We must receive a spark from his life of fulfilment.)

The founding father of this 'great institution' (President K.R. Narayanan's phrase in his condolence letter to Sisir's wife, Mrs Krishna Bose) is no more. But we can take solace from the words Rabindranath Tagore spoke about his father Debendranath Tagore in one of his Santiniketan lectures: '*Mrityur dwarai sei mahapurush tanr jeebanke sampurnabhabe uthsarga korechhen—tanr samasta badha dur hoye gechhe—ei jeebanke niye amader kono samsarik prayojaner tuchchata nei, kono loukik o samayik sambandher kshudrata nei. Tanr shange kebal ekti matro sampurna jog hoyechhe, se hochhe amriter jog. Mrityui ei amritake prakash kare.*' (It is through death that this great spirit has completely dedicated his life to us. All barriers have been broken. This life of ours is no longer constrained by any worldly trifle, nor the insignificance of any mundane or temporal relationship. We have only one complete connection with him—the tie of immortality. It is death which reveals this immortality.)

If I may take the liberty of paraphrasing Rabindranath a little: '*Ekdin . . . tini ekla amritajeebaner deeksha grahan korechhilen, sedinkar sambad khub alpa lokei jenechhilo . . . tanr ekdiner sei eklar deeksha aaj amra sakale mile grahan korbar adhikari hoyechhi. Sei adhikarke amra sarthak kore jabo.*' (One day he had alone received initiation into this life immortal; very few people knew of that day's conversation. The sacrament that was given to him alone on that day is to be shared by all of us today. We pledge to fulfil that responsibility.)

Let me conclude with that pledge in Dr Sisir Kumar Bose's own words:[3]

---

3 Translated from the Bengali poem 'Kaj Chalchhe' by Sumantra Bose.

THE WORK GOES ON

It happened on a winter afternoon,
I was called, bidding me to sit beside him,
He asked, I have some work,
Can you do it?
He looked with a serene, quiet, intent gaze,
Hoping for my answer,
What could I say?
What work? Post a letter?
Draft a telegram?
Or take care of a guest?
No, a secret task, to be his companion
On a secret journey, no one must know!
Except Ila.
Well, what was about to transpire?
I remembered Father saying
A couple of years ago
The boy has fallen under Subhas's spell,
Were his words coming true!
That was the commencement of work, the work goes on,
It will go on.

SUGATA BOSE

Acknowledgements

The editors wish to thank Professor Krishna Bose, M.P., and Professor Leonard A. Gordon for their editorial advice, Mr Kartic Chakraborty for secretarial assistance, the late Mr Naga Sundaram for archival support, and Manohar Mandal and Munshi for unstinted practical help in running the Bureau's publication division. For help in gathering material included in this volume we are grateful to the late Emilie Schenkl, the late Naomi Vetter, the late Alberto Quaroni, the late Dr Alexander Werth, Dr Miloslav Krasa, and other friends in Europe.

We take this opportunity once again to express our deep appreciation to Netaji's wife Emilie Schenkl and their daughter Anita Pfaff for having generously assigned the copyright in Netaji's works to the Netaji Research Bureau.

Introduction

On the night of 16–17 January 1941, Subhas Chandra Bose secretly left his Elgin Road home in Calcutta and was driven by his nephew Sisir in a Wanderer motor car up to Gomoh railway junction in Bihar. Before his departure he wrote a few post-dated letters to be mailed by Sisir on his return to Calcutta in order to give the British the false impression that he was still at home. Volume 11 of his Collected Works opens with one such letter written to his political colleague Hari Vishnu Kamath, who was then in prison. 'I will be back in jail very soon,' Subhas Chandra Bose wrote to cover the trail of his escape, 'because there are two cases going on against me.' Two years later, on the eve of setting out on a perilous submarine journey from Europe to Asia on 8 February 1943, he wrote a touching letter in Bengali for his elder brother Sarat Chandra Bose, which forms the last item in this volume: 'Today once again I am embarking on the path of danger. But this time towards home. I may not see the end of the road. If I meet with any such danger, I will not be able to send you any further news in this life. That is why today I am leaving my news here—it will reach you in due time. I have married here and I have a daughter. In my absence please show my wife and daughter the love that you have given me throughout your life.'

Between these two journeys lies a most difficult, daring and controversial phase in the life of India's foremost anti-colonial revolutionary. The writings and broadcasts of this period cover a broad range of topics including the nature and course of the Second World War, the need to distinguish between India's internal and external policy in the context of the international war crisis, plans for a final armed assault against British colonial rule in India, dismay at and criticism of Germany's invasion of the Soviet Union, the hypocrisy of Anglo-American notions of freedom and democracy, the role of Japan in East and Southeast Asia, the reasons for rejecting the Cripps offer of 1942, support for Mahatma Gandhi and the Quit India movement later that year, as well as reflections on future problems of reconstruction in free India. Several of these were printed in *Azad Hind*, the official bi-monthly journal of the Netaji's Free India Centre in Europe, now preserved in the archives of Netaji Research Bureau.[1]

Subhas Chandra Bose had left Calcutta in the guise of Mohammed Ziauddin, a Muslim insurance agent of north India travelling around on business. He took the Delhi-Kalka Mail from Gomoh to Delhi and the Frontier Mail on to Peshawar, where he was received by Mian Akbar Shah. On 26 January 1941, the day it was revealed in Calcutta that Subhas could not be found, he managed to cross the British Indian frontier into tribal territory.[2] Escorted by Bhagat Ram Talwar, he walked and hitch-hiked his way across difficult terrain pretending to be a deaf and mute pilgrim until he reached Kabul on 31 January 1941. There he was stuck for more than a month and a half until the Italian Legation arranged to let him travel as Orlando Mazzotta via Moscow to Berlin.

During his agonizing wait in Kabul during February and March 1941 he wrote a lengthy political tract which is often referred to as his 'Kabul thesis'. Employing the analytical tool of Hegelian dialectics, he argued the need for a Leftist Antithesis to a Rightist Thesis in each phase of history to be resolved in a higher Synthesis. Interestingly, he suggested that Gandhi in his 'Young India' phase of 1920–2 represented the Leftist Antithesis to the Rightist Thesis represented by moderate constitutionalism. He reiterated the two criteria for 'genuine Leftism' in Indian politics—uncompromising anti-imperialism in the current

---

[1] This remarkable publication in German and English was edited by Pandit K.A. Bhatta and carried quite fascinating articles written by a number of talented young men Netaji had gathered around him in addition to his own statements and broadcasts. Netaji's broadcasts were also recorded and transcribed by officials of the British government of India. Someone with access to these transcripts compiled several of the broadcasts under the pseudonym 'Arun' and published them in 1946 under the title *Testament of Subhas Bose*, preserved in the library of Netaji Research Bureau. These transcripts are now available in the Defence Department files of the National Archives of India. In cases of discrepancy between the versions in *Azad Hind* and the British government's transcripts of the same speeches, we have accorded precedence to *Azad Hind*.

Netaji also wrote the second part of his book *The Indian Struggle* covering the period 1935–42 at this time. This has been published as Sisir K. Bose and Sugata Bose (eds), *Netaji Collected Works Volume 2 The India Struggle, 1920–1942* (Calcutta: Netaji Research Bureau and Delhi: Oxford University Press, 1997).

[2] For the full story see Sisir Kumar Bose, *The Great Escape* (Calcutta: Netaji Research Bureau, 3rd edition, 2000).

phase and socialist reconstruction in the next. Having abandoned his fledgling pressure group within the Congress—the Forward Bloc—in the pursuit of the larger armed struggle, he could merely hope that '[h]istory will separate the chaff from the grain—the pseudo-Leftists from the genuine Leftists'. He claimed that his Forward Bloc had 'saved the Congress from stagnation and death', helped 'bring the Congress back to the path of struggle, however inadequately' and 'stimulated the intellectual and ideological progress of the Congress'. He asserted that 'in fulness of time' it would succeed in 'establishing Leftist ascendancy in the Congress so that the future progress of the latter (the Congress) may continue unhampered'. This handwritten thesis dated 22 March 1941 was delivered by Bhagat Ram Talwar to Sarat Chandra Bose and Sisir Kumar Bose at their Woodburn Park residence in Calcutta on 31 March 1941. It is now preserved in the archives of Netaji Research Bureau.

'You will be surprised to get this letter from me,' he wrote to Emilie Schenkl on 3 April 1941, 'and even more surprised to know that I am writing this from Berlin.'[3] He had flown in to the German capital from Moscow the previous afternoon. Bose went to Europe in 1941 primarily in order to gain access to Indian soldiers in the British Indian Army who were prisoners-of-war in the hands of Germany and Italy. He had long believed that the subversion of the loyalty of the Indian soldiers to the Raj and its replacement with a new loyalty to the Indian nation had to be a crucial part of the anti-imperialist movement. What is less well known is that Bose at this time had also a strong personal reason to want to go to Europe. He had written to Emilie on 21 June 1939, to 'please wait till August—probably I will come then to Gastein [Bad Gastein, their favourite Austrian resort]'. And then again on 6 July 1939: 'I must take a month's holiday at least—but I do not know if the holiday will begin in the middle of August or the beginning of September.' The outbreak of the War in September 1939 had put paid to all these plans. But now in the throes of the War Subhas and Emilie were able to

---

[3] Subhas Chandra Bose to Emilie Schenkl, 3 April 1941, in *Netaji Collected Works Volume 7 Letters to Emilie Schenkl 1934–1942* (Calcutta: Netaji Research Bureau and Delhi: Oxford University Press, 1994), p. 216. The letters to Emilie Schenkl of this period are not included in this volume since they have already been published in the special Volume 7.

share a brief period of home life together at Sophienstrasse 7 in the Charlottenburg neighbourhood of Berlin. Subhas Chandra Bose would, of course, continue to make personal sacrifices to serve the cause of his country.

Bose had already spoken of his plan of an Indian Revolution to Alberto Quaroni, the Italian diplomat in Kabul, who facilitated his journey to Europe. On 9 April 1941 he submitted a detailed memorandum with an explanatory note to the German Government setting out the work to be done in Europe, Afghanistan, the Tribal Territory and India. He concluded by pointing out that the 'overthrow of British power in India can, in its last stages, be materially assisted by Japanese foreign policy in the Far East.' He wrote with prescience 'A defeat of the British Navy in the Far East including the smashing up of the Singapore base,' will automatically weaken British military strength and prestige in India.' However, he felt that a prior agreement between the Soviet Union and Japan would both pave the way for a settlement with China and free up Japan to move confidently against the British in Southeast Asia. In a supplementary memorandum on 3 May 1941, he asked the Axis Powers to make a clear declaration of policy regarding the freedom of India and the Arab countries. He also discussed four possible routes for opening up a channel of communication between Germany and India among which he favoured the one going through Russia and Afghanistan. An armed thrust from the traditional northwesterly direction, he believed, would greatly help India's unarmed freedom-fighters at home. He communicated with his comrades at home through messages transmitted via Kabul and the Japanese Consulate in Calcutta which stayed in touch with Sarat Chandra Bose.

Before implementing any of his plans, Subhas Chandra Bose demanded an unambiguous and unequivocal declaration by the Tripartite Powers recognizing Indian independence. He wrote up a draft of such a declaration himself in the latter half of May 1941 and tried his best to get the German and Italian governments to issue it publicly. Nearly a year later, on 5 May 1942, Bose was able to persuade Mussolini to agree to such a Tripartite declaration in favour of Indian independence, but the Germans gave various excuses for delaying it.[4]

---

[4] See Leonard A. Gordon, *Brothers against the Raj: A Biography of Indian Nationalists Sarat and Subhas Chandra Bose* (New York: Columbia University Press, 1990), p. 483.

Bose was on one of his earlier visits to Rome when Germany invaded the Soviet Union on 22 June 1941. He was utterly dismayed by this turn of events, as it upset all his plans. He told the German Foreign Office in clear terms that 'the Indian people felt definitely that Germany was the aggressor'. In a letter to the German Foreign Minister von Ribbentrop on 15 August 1941, he stressed that without a declaration regarding Indian independence, 'the nearer the German armies move towards India, the more hostile will the Indian people become towards Germany.' *'The march of the German troops towards the East,'* he warned von Ribbentrop, *'will be regarded as the approach not of a friend, but of an enemy'.*

Yet perseverance in adversity was a quality that Subhas Chandra Bose possessed in full measure. With the help of Indian exiles in different parts of Europe, including students, he set up a Free India Centre, and from among Indian soldiers he raised an Indian Legion. Talented young Indians of different ideological persuasions, but all committed to the goal of India's freedom, joined him to craft in microcosm the future free India of his dreams. Among them were A.C.N. Nambiar, Abid Hasan, N.G. Swamy, N.G. Ganpuley, M.R. Vyas, P.B. Sharma, Pramode Sengupta, J.K. Banerji, A.M. Sultan, Habibur Rahman and Girija Mookerjee. India's national greeting 'Jai Hind' was coined at this time. Special efforts were made to unite all the religious communities in the common struggle.

Japan's entry into the War and its rapid advance across Southeast Asia against European colonial powers opened up new strategic possibilities for Netaji. The fall of Singapore on 15 February 1942, provided the occasion for Subhas Chandra Bose to discard his identity as Orlando Mazzotta and make his first open broadcast to India on 19 February 1942. After more than a year his countrymen heard his voice: 'This is Subhas Chandra Bose speaking to you over the Azad Hind Radio.' 'The fall of Singapore', he declared, 'means the collapse of the British Empire, the end of the iniquitous regime which it has symbolised and the dawn of a new era in Indian history ... Through India's liberation will Asia and the world move forward towards the larger goal of human emancipation.' As the Japanese forces took Rangoon from the British, he hailed the prospect of Burmese freedom. He derided British propaganda that India was under threat of enemy attack and that its frontiers, therefore, were at Suez and Hongkong which had to be defended with Indian troops. India, he pointed out, had 'no imaginary Wavellian frontiers', only 'a national geographical boundary determined by Providence and nature'. Having brought 'India into the war' in September 1939, the British were now trying to bring 'the war into India'.

In March 1942 British news agencies reported that Subhas Chandra Bose had been killed in an aircrash on his way to attend a conference in Tokyo. The report was immediately contradicted by Netaji himself in a broadcast on 25 March 1942, in which he said 'my death is perhaps an instance of wishful thinking'. He warned the Indian people to be wary of British divisive policies of the sort that had been deployed in Ireland and Palestine. In a series of broadcasts in spring 1942 he excoriated Sir Stafford Cripps for donning the imperialist mantle and urged the Indian people and leaders to contemptuously reject the offer of dominion status after the War's end. He welcomed the Japanese premier Tojo's promise of 'India for the Indians'. Netaji had successfully negotiated with the German Government that the broadcasts of the Azad Hind Radio would not be subjected to any censorship. The broadcasts usually began with the lines—'To arms, to arms, The Heavens ring, With the clarion call, To freedom's fray' and ended with 'Our cause is just'.[5] In a candid broadcast on 1 May 1942, Bose said that he was 'not an apologist of the Tripartite Powers' and it was 'not [his] task to defend what they have done or may do in future'. He rebutted 'Britain's paid propagandists' and justified his own wartime strategy in the quest of India's liberation in these terms: *I need no credentials when I speak to my own people. My whole life, which has been one long, consistent and continuous record of uncompromising struggle against British Imperialism, is the best guarantee of my bona fides* . . . If the Britishers who are the past masters in the art of diplomacy and political seduction, have in spite of their best efforts, failed to tempt, corrupt or mislead me, no other power on earth can do so. All my life I have been a servant of India and till the last hours of my life I shall remain one. *My allegiance and my loyalty has ever been and will ever be to India* and to India alone, no matter in which part of the world I may live at any given time.

[5] See Krishna Bose, *Itihaser Sandhane* (Calcutta: Ananda Publishers, 1972 and 1998), p. 31.

He had absolutely no doubt where he should be located at that particular moment in world history. '[N]ow the time has come,' he wrote to von Ribbentrop on 22 May 1942, 'when the final effort should be made for achieving India's political emancipation. For this purpose, it is absolutely essential that I should be in the East. Only when I am there, shall I be able to direct the revolution along the right channels.'

At his one and only meeting with Hitler on 29 May 1942, he raised the issue of his 'journey to East Asia', 'motivated by the desire to find a point as close to India as possible, from where the Indian revolution could be directed'. Fortunately, the German Führer agreed with this proposal and promised logistical support for Bose to travel by submarine from Europe to Asia. Bose raised other issues, including Hitler's anti-Indian racist remarks in *Mein Kampf*. Hitler evaded the question saying that he had not wanted 'passive resistance for the Reich of the Indian pattern'. Bose was clearly unaware of the diabolical and murderous nature of the racism in the monster he was facing.

Netaji was also anxious to stress his ideological distance from the Axis Powers. He kept repeating that once freedom was won it would be 'the duty of the Indian people to decide what form of Government they desire and who should guide the future Indian state.' 'In this fateful hour in India's history,' he proclaimed in a key broadcast on 17 June 1942, 'it would be a grievous mistake to be carried away by ideological concerns alone. The internal politics of Germany or Italy or Japan do not concern us—they are the concern of the people of those countries.' He wanted Indians to 'differentiate between the internal and external policy of Free India'. 'While standing for full collaboration with the Tripartite Powers', he asserted, 'in the external sphere—I stand for absolute self-determination for India where her national affairs are concerned and I shall never tolerate any interference in the internal policy of the Free Indian State.' So far as socioeconomic problems were concerned, his views were 'exactly what they were when [he] was at home—and no one should make the mistake of concluding that external collaboration with the Tripartite Powers mean[t] acceptance of their domination or even of their ideology in [India's] internal affairs.' Once his task of liberating India was complete, he would once again call on Mahatma Gandhi as he had promised in his farewell talk with him in June 1940.

During the spring and summer of 1942 Mahatma Gandhi and Netaji drew closer in their aims and strategy in relation to the War and the final struggle for Indian independence. Netaji gave unstinted and enthusiastic support to Gandhiji as he moved towards launching the Quit India movement. Detailed instructions were broadcast to the insurgents on how to sustain the uprising and make it more effective. Having taken prominent part in all the Congress movements since 1921, Subhas Chandra Bose was disappointed not to be at home with his people in 1942, but promised that it would 'not be long before' he was at their side again. He correctly noted on 17 August 1942 that British colonial rule had been forced to rest on its ultimate coercive foundation:

> The whole world now sees that the velvet glove which ordinarily hides the mailed fist of Britain has now been cast away and brute force—naked and unashamed—rules over India. Behind the thick screen of gas, underneath the heavy blows of police batons, amid the continual whistle of bullets and the angry defiance of the injured and dying—the soul of India asks—'Where are the four freedoms?' The words float over the seven seas to all corners of the globe—but Washington does not reply. After a pause, the soul of India asks again—'Where is the Atlantic Charter which guaranteed to every nation its own Government?' This time Downing Street and White House reply simultaneously—'That Charter was not meant for India.'

Yet he probably knew that the Congress-led movement of 1942 had failed to enthuse all religious communities and regional peoples. He, therefore called upon progressive elements of the Muslim League, the Majlis-i-Ahrar, the Jamiat-ul-Ulema, the Azad Muslim League, the Akali Dal and, last but not least, the Krishak Praja Party of Bengal to form a broad-based patriotic front. He also underlined the importance of the peasantry in the sort of non-violent guerilla war being waged in India.

Even in the midst of war Netaji kept thinking and writing about the post-war reconstruction of free India. In a political essay titled 'Free India and Her Problems' he wrote it would be 'wrong to dogmatize from now about the form of the future Indian state'. He did say, however, that to begin with there will be 'a strong Central Government' and 'a well-organized, disciplined all-India party'. The state would 'guarantee complete religious and cultural freedom for individuals and groups'. 'When the new regime is stabilised and the state-machinery begins to function smoothly,' he explained, 'power will be decentralized and the provincial governments will be given more responsibility.' When an occasion presented itself, as it did on the foundation of the Indo-German Society in Hamburg on 11 September 1942, Subhas Chandra Bose spoke of the bonds of poetry and philosophy, rather than just of politics. Was he seeking refuge in the past world of Goethe and Schopenhauer, Ruckert and Schlegel, Max Muller and Deussen, away from the oppressive present of Nazi Germany?

Subhas Chandra Bose gave an important speech on the USA, Britain and India that was broadcast from Berlin on 15 October 1942. 'We thankfully recognize the fact,' he said, 'that a large section of the American people have sympathy for Indian independence, but unfortunately they are powerless to influence their own Government. So far as American official policy towards India is concerned, it is as imperialistic as that of Britain.' In early November Netaji travelled to Rome as arrangements had been made there for him to travel to Southeast Asia. Netaji's flight to Asia had to be called off at the last moment for either technical reasons or the possibility of a leak. Subhas and Emilie's daughter Anita was born in Vienna on 29 November 1942. Netaji travelled once more to Vienna in December to see his wife and new-born daughter. If his earlier plans of going to Asia had materialized, the revolutionary would have missed this joyous event in his personal life.

'My country calls me—my duty calls me—', Subhas Chandra Bose had written to Emilie Schenkl in March 1936, 'I must leave you and go back to my first love—my country.'[6] So it was to be again now, but in far more dangerous war conditions. 'I could do much more for my country,' Bose wrote to von Ribbentrop on 5 December 1942, exactly a week after his daughter's birth, 'if I could be somewhere near India.' He continued: 'I believe that it is technically possible for the German Government to help me to travel to the Far East—either by aeroplane or by submarine or by ship. There is a certain amount of risk undoubtedly

---

[6] Subhas Chandra Bose to Emilie Schenkl, 5 March 1936, in Sisir K. Bose and Sugata Bose (eds), *The Essential Writings of Netaji Subhas Chandra Bose* (Calcutta: Netaji Research Bureau and Delhi: Oxford University Press, 1997), p. 160.

in this undertaking, but so is there in every undertaking. That risk I shall gladly and voluntarily take. At the same time, I believe in my destiny and I therefore believe that this endeavour will succeed.'

By mid-January 1943 plans were finalized for his submarine journey to Asia. Emilie came to Berlin on 20 January to spend their last days together. Speeches were recorded to be broadcast during his travel. The one broadcast, on 1 March 1943, was not especially well done as it contained a long passage from an earlier speech. Another speech was commemorative of the anniversary of the Amritsar massacre on 13 April and could be broadcast without references to recent developments in the War.

Netaji made his final public appearance in Berlin at a big ceremony to observe Independence Day on 26 January 1943. The Independence Pledge of the Indian National Congress was read out. The 'very colourful and eminent gathering' of some 600 guests included the Grand Mufti of Jerusalem and Rashid Ali of Iraq. Netaji walked into the hall decorated with red tulips and white lilacs dressed in a black sherwani and addressed the assembly in German. An English recording of his speech was beamed simultaneously towards India. In a wide-ranging speech he said in a philosophical digression:

> To us, life is one long unending wave. It is God manifesting himself in the infinite variety of creation. It is 'Leela'—an eternal play of forces. In this cosmic interplay of forces—there is not only sunshine, but there is also darkness. There is not only joy, but there is also sorrow. There is not only a rise, but there is also a fall. If we do not lose faith in ourselves and in our divinity— we shall move on through darkness, sorrow and degradation towards renewed sunshine, joy and progress.

Leaving a Bengali letter for his 'Mejda' Sarat Chandra Bose in the hands of his wife Emilie on 8 February 1943, Netaji Subhas Chandra boarded a submarine at Kiel harbour along with his trusted aide Abid Hasan to ride the wave towards the fulfilment of his and his country's destiny.

SUGATA BOSE

1

A Post-dated Letter[1]

To Hari Vishnu Kamath

38/2 Elgin Road
Calcutta, 18.1.41

My dear Kamath,

I was delighted to have your letter after my release and to know that you are well and in good spirits.

I have improved since my release—but the progress is slow as my vitality has been lowered. However, there is no cause for anxiety—it will only take time.

I do not know what company you have there. If you have any associates, please give them my most cordial greetings.

I shall be back in jail very soon, because there are two cases going on against me.

With love and cordial greetings and sincerest good wishes,

Yours affly,
SUBHAS C. BOSE

H.V. Kamath, Esq.

---

[1] Subhas Chandra Bose left a number of post-dated letters to be mailed after his escape on the night of 16–17 January 1941. He left his home at 38/2 Elgin Road, Calcutta, at 1.35 a.m. on 17th January 1941. He was driven by his nephew Sisir Kumar Bose to Gomoh railway station in Bihar. This letter to his close political associate Hari Vishnu Kamath, then in prison, is one of several that were mailed to give the British the impression that he was still at home.

2

Forward Bloc: Its Justification

THE KABUL THESIS, 22 MARCH 1941[1]

The evolution of a Movement is analogous to that of a tree. It grows from within and at every stage it throws out new branches, so that there may be ever increasing progress. When no fresh branches sprout forth, the Movement may be presumed to be in a process of decay or death.

While every Movement draws its sustenance from the soil from which it springs, it also assimilates nourishment coming from outside—from the atmosphere, environment, etc. Internal sustenance and external nourishment are both necessary for a living Movement.

When the main stream of a Movement begins to stagnate, but there is still vitality in the Movement as a whole—a Left Wing invariably appears. The main function of the Left Wing is to stimulate progress when there is danger of it being arrested. The appearance of a Left Wing is followed by a conflict between it and the main stream, which now becomes the Right Wing. This conflict is a temporary phase and through it a higher stage is reached, when the conflict is resolved. The solution of the conflict takes place through some sort of agreement or adjustment, whereby the Left Wing begins to dominate the Movement as a whole. Thus the Left Wing becomes, in time, the main stream of the Movement.

One may describe this process of evolution in philosophical language by saying that the 'Thesis' throws up its 'Antithesis', and the conflict between the two is resolved in a 'Synthesis'. This 'Synthesis', in its turn, becomes the 'Thesis' of the next stage of evolution.

[1] This thesis was written by Subhas Chandra Bose in Kabul during his great escape in March 1941. The manuscript, dated 22 March 1941, was delivered by Bhagat Ram Talwar to Sarat Chandra Bose and Sisir Kumar Bose in Calcutta on 31 March 1941. It is often referred to as the Kabul Thesis.

This process of evolution—called the 'dialectical process'—if properly comprehended, can give a new meaning and significance to the developments that have taken place within the Indian National Congress during the last few decades. We shall herein study the Gandhi Movement from the dialectical point of view.

We may observe at this stage that it would be an error to suppose that conflicts inside a Movement are unhealthy or undesirable under all circumstances. It would indeed be more correct to say that conflicts which arise from the logic of history are essential to progress whether in the sphere of thought or in the sphere of action.

There is no fixed rule as to when a Movement or a particular phase of it should lose its dynamism and begin to stagnate. So long as it can assimilate from outside and go on creating something new, decay cannot set in.

To come now to a study of the Gandhi Movement. By 1919, after the close of the World War, a new situation arose in India and with it, new problems. The official Indian National Congress could not face this situation as it had lost its dynamism altogether, and a Left Wing was clearly necessary if the entire Congress was not to stagnate and die. At this juncture a Left Wing appeared in the form of the Gandhi Movement. Conflict ensued for a time and the old leaders were driven out of the Congress or voluntarily withdrew. Ultimately, a 'Synthesis' took place. The Congress accepted the tenets of Mahatma Gandhi and the Left Wing then became the official Congress.

In 1920, Gandhiism took possession of the Indian National Congress and for two decades it has maintained its hold. This has been possible, not merely because of Mahatma Gandhi's personality but also because of his capacity to assimilate other ideas and policies. But for the latter factor, Gandhiism would have ceased to dominate the Congress long ago. During its twenty years' domination of the Congress, whenever revolts appeared, the Gandhi Movement took the wind out of their sails by accepting many of their ideas and policies—and only recently has it shown signs of failing to adapt itself to the changing environment. For instance, when the Swarajya Party arose in 1923, the conflict that followed continued only for a time.

At the Cawnpore Congress in 1925, the Swarajist policy of carrying non-co-operation inside the Legislatures was accepted by the Gandhiites and was thereupon adopted by the Congress as a whole.

Again in December 1928, at the Calcutta Congress there was a revolt against Gandhiism sponsored by the Independence League on the issue of Independence. Mahatma Gandhi then advocated Dominion Status and he fought and defeated our resolution on Independence. But a year later, at the Lahore Congress, he himself moved the resolution declaring that henceforth Independence was to be the goal of the Indian National Congress.

By this process of assimilation, the Gandhi Movement was able to maintain its progressive character and prevent the emergence of any big Left Wing development. There was a temporary setback after the Gandhi–Irwin Pact in March 1931, but Gandhiji recovered lost ground when he launched Satyagraha or Civil Disobedience in January 1932.

The failure of this Civil Disobedience Movement and its abandonment in May 1933, created a new situation which gave birth to a fresh revolt—this time from the Right. Disappointed at the failure of the Movement, a large section of Gandhiites urged the revival of the parliamentary programme which had been scrapped by them at the Lahore Congress in December 1929, before the launching of Satyagraha by Mahatma Gandhi in 1930. Gandhiji surrendered to this demand in 1934, ostensibly because he had no alternative plan for the Congress. This incident was an indication that stagnation in the Gandhi Movement had set in and this was confirmed when a big Left Wing revolt arose through the medium of the Congress Socialist Party which was inaugurated in 1934, almost contemporaneously with the swing towards parliamentarianism.

The Gandhi Movement did not lose its elasticity and adaptability in a day and the attitude of the Gandhiites towards the Congress Socialists and other Leftists remained benevolent on the whole in 1934 and after. As a matter of fact, the Congress Socialists were offered seats on the Congress Working Committee in 1936, 1937 and 1938. (They did not accept the offer in 1938.) In January 1938, the Gandhiites, at the instance of Mahatma Gandhi himself, supported my candidature for the Congress Presidentship. And at the Haripura Congress in February 1938, when I was to nominate the working Committee for the year, Gandhiji was clearly of opinion that there could be no objection to having Socialists on the Working Committee.

A distinct—and what has still remained inexplicable—change in Mahatma Gandhi's attitude came in September 1938, after a meeting of the All-India Congress Committee at Delhi, at which there was a walk-out of the Left Wingers over a controversial issue. It was then that one heard Gandhiji saying that there could be no compromise with the Leftists in conducting the affairs of the Congress. A few months later, in January 1939, he gave proof of the same mentality by opposing my re-election as Congress President.

Since September 1938, Gandhiism has tended to become increasingly static and hide-bound. At the Haripura Congress in February of the same year, the two most important resolutions passed were on the questions of Federation and the coming War. Though the resolution on Federation was one of uncompromising opposition, throughout that year the air was thick with rumours that negotiations for a compromise between the Gandhiites and the British Government were going on behind the scenes. My attitude of uncompromising hostility towards Federation was the first item in the Gandhian charge-sheet against my Presidentship. The second item was what the Gandhiites regarded as my unduly friendly attitude towards the Leftists. The third item in the charge-sheet was my sponsoring and subsequent inauguration of the National Planning Committee which, in the view of the Gandhiites, would give a fillip to large-scale production at the sacrifice of village industries, the revival of which was a very important item in the Gandhian constructive programme. The next charge against me was that I advocated an early resumption of the national struggle for Independence, to be preceded by an ultimatum to the British Government.

By September 1938, any intelligent person could have foreseen that in future the relations between the Gandhiites and the Leftists would cease to be cordial. As already indicated above, Gandhiji himself gave a frank expression to the change in his mentality. Furthermore, it became clear to esoteric circles in the Congress at the time of the Munich Pact that in the event of a War-crisis overtaking India in the future—an open rupture between the Gandhiites and the Leftists would become unavoidable. It is true that from 1927 (Madras Congress) to 1938—the War-policy of the Congress was clearly enunciated in successive annual sessions of the Congress and one would not under ordinary circumstances have expected any divergence of opinion, not to speak of a rupture, among Congressmen on the war issue. Nevertheless, discussions among important Congress leaders during the international crisis preceding the Munich Pact left no room for doubt that the Gandhiites cherished no enthusiasm for the war-resolutions passed by preceding sessions of the Congress and they would not hesitate to circumvent them should they find it necessary or convenient to do so. Now the two questions on which the Leftists were tremendously keen and on which they would not countenance any compromise were those of Federation and the coming War. Consequently, the vacillating and compromising attitude of the Gandhiites on these two issues presaged a breach between them and the Leftists in the days to come.

Though the Munich Pact staved off the war in Europe for the time being, students of International Politics could not but feel that the War was nevertheless unavoidable and imminent. The conviction began thereafter to grow within me that in view of the international situation, the British Government would give up the idea of forcing Federation down the throats of the Indian people. Federation being no longer a live issue for the Indians, it was necessary for them to decide about their future political plans. Since the much-expected battle royal on the Federation issue was off, how were they to continue the fight for Independence?

In November 1938, when I began my North India tour, I put forward a solution of this problem. I urged that it was no use waiting for the Government to take the initiative against the Indian people. Federation being dead, at least for the time being, and war being ahead of us in the not-distant future, it was time for Congress to take the initiative. The proper method for doing so would be to send an ultimatum to the British Government demanding Independence within a certain period and start preparing the country for a national struggle. This idea was widely propagated by us from November onwards and it came before the Tripuri Congress in March 1939, in the form of a resolution—but it was defeated at the instance of the Gandhiites. That resolution stated, inter alia, that after the ultimatum was sent to the British Government, a period of six months would be given within which a definite reply was called for. Six months after the Tripuri Congress when war broke out in Europe, the political wisdom underlying our resolution was admitted even by the Gandhiites who were so much against us at Tripuri.

Soon after War was declared in Europe, Mahatma Gandhi, who was then the unofficial Dictator of the Congress, issued a public statement advocating unconditional co-operation with Great Britain in the prosecution of the War. The resolutions repeatedly passed by the Congress during a period of eleven years were conveniently forgotten. (Federation was officially postponed by the Government after the War broke out).

Since 1938, the issues on which we Leftists have found ourselves at loggerheads with the Gandhiites and on which no compromise has been possible—are the resumption of the national struggle for Independence and the correct war-policy of the Indian people. It is to be noted that till November 1940, Mahatma Gandhi consistently declared in private and in public, that any Satyagraha or Civil Disobedience was out of the question and that anybody who launched such a movement would be doing harm to his country. It is true that in November 1940, individual Satyagraha was started under his auspices. But as Gandhiji himself has declared and as we all know very well, it is not a mass struggle for the attainment of Independence. As responsible British officials in India and in England have already declared, this movement has not embarrassed the British Government to any appreciable degree. In conformity with his desire that Great Britain should win the War, Mahatma Gandhi has refrained from creating an embarrassing situation for the Government which a mass struggle for winning Independence would naturally have done.

In September 1939, Mahatma Gandhi advocated unconditional co-operation with Great Britain in the prosecution of the War, but in November 1940, he demanded liberty to carry on anti-war propaganda. Since 1938, he consistently denounced all attempts to resume the national struggle for Independence, but in November 1940, he modified that stand so far as to actually launch the Individual Civil Disobedience Movement. Would it not be a moot-question to ask as to what could explain this change however small? And would it be wrong to say that this change has been due entirely to the pressure from the Left?

That Gandhiji could, even at his present age, alter a position consistently and tenaciously advocated and upheld by him for a fairly long period—though this change may be due to pressure and be only partial—is evidence of his adaptability and mobility. Nevertheless it is not adequate for the needs of the times. We are now living in the 'Blitzkrieg' period of history and if we do not move with the times, we shall have to go under. So far, Gandhiji has been unable to prove by his action that he can keep abreast of the times and lead his nation—and this accords with our belief which we have already stated that the Gandhi Movement is becoming static and hide-bound.

The uncompromising attitude towards heterodox thought which the Gandhiites have been evincing since September 1938, and their increasing desire and endeavour to expel dynamic and radical elements from the Congress—not only prove that they are losing their adaptability and mobility but will, like a vicious circle, make them more and more static. The various nonpolitical organisations which Gandhiji has started for the Gandhiites (e.g, the All-India Spinners Association, the Gandhi Seva Sangh, the Harijan Sevak Sangh, the All-India Village Industries Association, the Hindi Prachar Samity, etc.) will also undermine the political dynamism of the Gandhi Movement in future by creating non-political vested interests, as it has already been doing. And more than anything else, peaceful parliamentary life and ministerial office has been, and will be, the political grave of Gandhiism.

Whatever revolutionary fervour the Gandhi Movement had, was sapped more by the acceptance of ministerial office than by any other factor. It would be no exaggeration to say that under the influence of this factor, a large number of Congressmen have definitely turned from the thorny path of Revolution to the rosy path of Constitutionalism. Congress Ministries in the provinces were formed in 1937 and neo-Constitutionalism reared its head in a menacing form within the Congress in 1938. Ever since then, the main task of Leftism has been to fight this 'Frankenstein' created by the Congress itself. How to stem this drift towards Constitutionalism, how to create afresh a revolutionary mentality among the people in place of the neo-constitutionalist mentality, how to face the war-crisis in a bold and adequate manner, how to bring the Congress back to the path of uncompromising National Struggle and how ultimately to establish Leftist ascendancy in the Congress—these have been the main problems for the Leftists since 1938.

The Gandhi Movement today has become a victim of not only Constitutionalism but also of Authoritarianism. A certain amount of Authoritarianism is permissible and natural in a militant organisation. But the excessive Authoritarianism that one finds today is traceable to the same cause as Constitutionalism. Since the acceptance of Ministerial office, the Gandhiites have had a taste of power and they are anxious to monopolise it for themselves in future. What has been going on within the Congress of late, is 'power politics', though of a sham kind. The fountainhead of this 'power politics' is Wardha. It is the aim of this 'power-politics' to beat down all opposition within the Congress so that the Gandhiites may comfortably rule the roost for all time. But this game will not succeed. Real power has yet to come and it will never come if we travel along the safe path of Constitutionalism. It is certainly possible for the Gandhiites to expel all discordant elements from the Congress and make it a close preserve. But that does not mean that they will be able to win liberty for India. And without real power, there cannot be real 'power-politics'. What we see therefore today is sham 'power politics'.

Personally I would have no objection to the Gandhiites trying to monopolise power for themselves or acting in an authoritarian manner, if they had been a revolutionary force. But unfortunately, Gandhiism has ceased to be revolutionary. There is no hope that it will succeed in carrying the nation towards its goal of national independence. Consequently, the more our Gandhiite friends try to consolidate their power, position and influence, the more stagnation they will bring into the Congress. Liberal doses of disciplinary action against non-conformists may make the Congress a more homogeneous body than at present, but that process will only create more enemies outside and in the end will strike at the 'mass-basis' of the Congress and undermine the hold which the Congress has over the country at large.

The efforts of the Gandhiites to consolidate themselves is nothing else than 'Right-consolidation' within the Congress. This had gone on slowly for a long time and unnoticed, till it was accentuated with the acceptance of Ministerial office. When the danger was detected and the Leftists began to organise in self-defence, a furore arose in Gandhian circles. For the latter, self-consolidation, i.e., Right-consolidation, was right and natural; but Left-consolidation was a crime.

Ever since Gandhiism has begun to stagnate and a big Left Wing has emerged in opposition to it, the Gandhiites have become Rightists and Gandhian-consolidation has come to mean Right-consolidation.

Philosophically speaking, Right-consolidation is the 'thesis' which demands its 'anti-thesis' in Left-consolidation. Without this 'antithesis' and the conflict following in its wake, no further progress is possible. All those who believe in progress and desire it, should therefore actively assist in this task of Left-consolidation and should be prepared for the conflict resulting therefrom. For bringing about Left-consolidation, the Forward Bloc was born in May 1939, soon after a momentous Session of the All-India Congress Committee in Calcutta, at which I tendered my resignation of the office of President.

Left-consolidation could have been achieved in either of the following ways:

(i) By forming one party and rallying all the Leftist elements therein. This, however, was not possible because several parties claiming to be Leftists, already existed, and they were not prepared to liquidate themselves in favour of one Party.

(ii) By organising a new Bloc which all Leftists and existing Leftist parties would join, while retaining the separate identity of their respective parties, if they so desired.

This was the first aim and endeavour of the Forward Bloc when it was launched. It did not want to start rivalry with the existing Leftist parties, not did it want to undermine any of them. If the Bloc's proposal had been accepted and all Leftist parties had joined the Forward Bloc, while retaining their separate identity—Left-consolidation would have been easily and promptly achieved and the Rightists would have been faced with a formidable force. But unfortunately for the Leftist cause, this also was not possible, because some of the existing Leftist parties prohibited their members from joining the newly formed Forward Bloc. What accounted for this inexplicable attitude on the part of these parties, need not be discussed here.

(iii) In the above circumstances, a fresh attempt at Left-consolidation was made in the following manner. The existing Leftist parties and the Forward Bloc agreed among themselves to form a new Committee to be called the Left-consolidation Committee. This Committee was to function as the organ of the entire Left—but it would act only when there was unanimity among the component elements of the Left-consolidation Committee.

The Left-consolidation Committee was formed in Bombay in June 1939, and the effect was immediate and striking. For the first time, the entire Left presented a united and organised front at the meeting of the All-India Congress Committee which was being held at the time. Though numerically in a minority, the Leftists were thereby able to prevent several changes being enacted in the Congress constitution, on which the Rightists were known to be very keen. That meeting of the All-India Congress Committee was a moral victory for the Leftists and on the surface, it seemed to augur well for the Leftist Cause.

But on the 9th July 1939, the first blow at the Left-consolidation Committee was struck and by Mr M.N. Roy. The Committee had decided to observe the 9th July as an All-India Day for protesting against two resolutions of an anti-Left character which had been passed by the All-India Congress Committee at its Bombay meeting in June in the teeth of Leftist opposition. The Congress President, Babu Rajendra Prasad, issued a statement in July calling upon Leftists to abandon the All-India Day on pain of disciplinary action. As a result of this threat, Mr M.N. Roy made an announcement at the eleventh hour to the effect that his Party, the Radical League, would not participate in the observance of the All-India Day. He also telegraphed to Pandit Jawaharlal Nehru requesting him to use his influence with the Congress Socialist Party and dissuade them from participating in the All-India Day. Since Mr M.N. Roy was then looked upon as a Leftist leader and his Radical League was one of the component units of the Left-consolidation Committee, his action amounted to a betrayal of the Leftist cause and was warmly acclaimed by the Rightists.

Though handicapped by the defection of the Radical League, the other members of the Committee carried on as usual, and their determination to hold together increased when the War situation overtook the country in September 1939. But in October, a new crisis appeared when the leaders of the Congress Socialist Party announced in Lucknow that in future their Party would act on its own and would not follow the direction of the Left-consolidation Committee. Nevertheless, consultations between them and other members of the Committee continued for a time.

The next blow struck at the Left-consolidation Committee was in December 1939, when a breach between the Forward Bloc and the National Front took place. The relations between the two had hitherto remained close and cordial. For instance, when the Anti-Imperialist Conference was held at Nagpur in October, on the eve of the meeting of the Congress Working Committee at Wardha, the National Front enthusiastically participated in it, along with the Forward Bloc, Kishan Sabha and others, though the Congress Socialists from other provinces outside C.P. and Berar did not. And after the Congress Socialists withdrew from the L.C.C. later in October at Lucknow the Forward Bloc and National Front continued to collaborate. It was, however, brought to the notice of the Forward Bloc that the National Front had been carrying on propaganda against the former, while outwardly collaborating on the Left-consolidation Committee. What is more, it appeared that in an official journal of the National Front, an official article had appeared painting the Forward Bloc as a counter-revolutionary organisation and adversely criticising it in many ways. This matter was brought up at a meeting of the leaders of the Bloc and of the National Front held in Calcutta in December 1939. The latter refused to disown the above article or to withdraw it. Thereupon they were told by the Forward Bloc leaders that a 'counter-revolutionary' organisation could not collaborate with the National Front on the Left-consolidation Committee.

The attitude of the National Front leaders showed that they wanted to use the platform of the L.C.C. for popularising their organisation, while carrying on reprehensible propaganda, both secret and open, against the component unit of the Committee.

When the breach took place at Calcutta in December 1939, the National Front openly informed the Forward Bloc that if a national struggle was launched by the latter independently of the Congress, the former would openly denounce it and resist it.

This breach was further accentuated by a conflict between the Bengal Branch of the Forward Bloc and of the National Front over some other issues.

Even before the Left Consolidation Committee was started, there was in operation something like a L.C.C. in Bengal. As a result, the Leftists were in an over-whelming majority in the Bengal Provincial Congress Committee, the dominant partner in the Leftist Combination being those who later on joined the Forward Bloc when it was formed. The Leftist Combination naturally became stronger when the Left Consolidation Committee was started on an All-India basis.

After the 9 July 1939, disciplinary action was taken against the President of the Bengal Provincial Congress Committee (i.e., myself) by the Congress Working Committee for participating in the All-India Day. This was resented by all the Leftists in the B.P.C.C. including the National Front and a united protest was made by them. It soon became apparent that the above action of the Working Committee was but the beginning of a long chain of unwarranted interference and persecution on the part of that Committee. All the Leftists in the B.P.C.C. then resolved not to submit meekly to the Working Committee but to continue their protest. After a few months, it became evident that their Working Committee was determined to go to any length, including their suspension of the valid B.P.C.C. and the setting up of an Ad Hoc Committee instead. At this stage the National Fronters in the B.P.C.C. began to show signs of weakness as well as reluctance to continue their attitude of protest against the high-handed action of the Working Committee. This was regarded by other Leftists as something like an act of betrayal in the midst of a grim fight and it looked as if the National Fronters were frightened at the prospect of disciplinary action. But the National Fronters wanted to cloak their real motive and they tried to side-track the issue by saying that instead of engaging in an organisational conflict with the Working Committee, the B.P.C.C. as a Leftist body should launch a struggle against the Government on the issue of Civil Liberty. The other Leftists were quite prepared to do this, but they wanted to continue their organisational protest against the Working Committee simultaneously. Ultimately, after a period of tension, an agreement was arrived at between the National Fronters and all the other Leftists in January 1940, whereby the B.P.C.C. was to launch a struggle on the issue of Civil Liberty and the National Fronters were to join the other Leftists in continuing the protest against the Working Committee. Towards the end of January 1940, the B.P.C.C. launched the movement as agreed upon and public meetings began to be held in defiance of the official ban. But after some time it was noticed that when the National Fronters held any public meeting, they did so after obtaining the permission of the authorities. In July 1940, when the B.P.C.C. launched the Holwell Monument Satyagraha, not only did the National Fronters not join it—but some of them actually opposed it. Furthermore, after the All-India Anti-Compromise Conference at Ramgarh in March 1940, when the Forward Bloc announced the launching of a nation-wide struggle, the National Fronters did their best to resist that move as well.

So much about participating in a struggle. With regard also to joining in the protest against the Congress High Command, the National Fronters did not fulfill their part of the agreement and they began to drop off. When the Working Committee in an un-warranted and illegal manner suspended the valid B.P.C.C. which had been dominated by the Leftists and set up an Ad Hoc Committee instead, the National Fronters quietly parted company with the other Leftists. The latter decided to ignore the fiat of the High Command and the valid B.P.C.C. continued to function. The National Fronters at first made a show of neutrality by declaring that they would not join either side. A little later, however, they began to apply to the Ad Hoc Committee for the recognition of their membership. Today they have cast off all sense of shame and openly declare that they cannot sever their connection with the Congress Working Committee.

The behaviour of the National Fronters in Bengal towards the Forward Blocers and other Leftists there, had repercussions in the All-India field and served to widen the breach between the two organisations which took place at Calcutta in December 1939, on All-India issues.

After the events of December 1939, all that remained of the Left Consolidation Committee was the Forward Bloc and the Kishan Sabha. Their collaboration became closer and closer with the passage of time. It was owing to their co-operation and initiative that the All-India Anti-Compromise Conference was held at Ramgarh, in March 1940, contemporaneously with the annual session of the Congress and proved to be such a remarkable success.

The question may very well be raised as to why the Forward Bloc was at all started and why the existing Leftist parties were not charged with the responsibility of bringing about Left-consolidation. The experiment was in fact tried but it failed and then there arose a situation in which it became imperative to start the Forward Bloc, if the Leftists were to be rallied under one banner and the menace of Right-consolidation was to be countered.

With the formation of the Congress Socialist Party, Radical League and similar organisations in 1934 and after, and the decision of the National Front to join the Congress—the Leftists in the Congress began to gain appreciably in influence and in numbers. This continued till 1937 but in 1938 the process suffered a check and it was quite noticeable at the Haripura Congress in February 1938. After Haripura, Leftists belonging to different parties began to put their heads together with a view to devising ways and means for increasing the Leftist strength. These efforts continued from February 1938 to April 1939. The proposal then was to form a Left Bloc and the Congress Socialist Party and the National Front were requested to take the lead in organising it. I took an active part in these efforts and many individuals like myself who had not till then joined any of the existing parties—pledged their support to the Leftist Bloc. Both the C.S.P. and the National Front at first took the idea of the Left Bloc with great enthusiasm, but they ultimately gave it up. Why they did so, remains a mystery to me up to the present day. Perhaps they thought that if the Left Bloc was organised and if it began to flourish—the importance of their respective parties would wane. Be that as it may, there is no doubt that if the Left Bloc had been launched in time, it would have taken the place of the Forward Bloc. The failure to start the Left Bloc belonged primarily to the C.S.P. and the N.F.

Now why did the existing parties fail to serve the Leftist cause adequately and why was a new organisation necessary? The answer evidently is that for some reason or other they failed to rally all those who should and could have been brought into the Leftist fold. Perhaps they were too keen on propagating Socialism—a thing of the future—whereas the immediate task was the widening and strengthening of the anti-imperialist front and an intensification of the anti-imperialist struggle. There was a large number of Congressmen who viewed with dismay the growth of Right-consolidation and the consequent drift towards Constitutionalism, following the acceptance of ministerial office in the provinces. They were naturally more interested in widening and strengthening the anti-imperialist front than in any thing else. It was with the help of these men that we could hope to resist the onslaught from the Right and establish Leftist ascendancy in the Congress. It had therefore been decided that the programme of the Left Bloc would be a minimum anti-imperialist programme, on the basis of which we could hope to rally all genuine anti-imperialists under one banner and give battle to the Rightists.

This was also our idea at the time we launched the Forward Bloc. Our immediate task was to fight the increasing drift towards Constitutionalism, reconvert the Congress into a revolutionary organisation and bring it back to the path of national struggle and prepare the country for the coming War crisis.

Since its birth, the Forward Bloc has developed greatly, along with changes in the Indian political scene. But it has failed to bring other parties together on one platform, as originally intended. Does that mean that there is no hope of Left-consolidation? No. It only means that Left-consolidation will be achieved by some other means.

A word is necessary here as to what exactly is meant by Leftism. When different individuals and organisations claim to be Leftists, how are we to decide who are—and who are not genuine Leftists? In the present political phase of Indian life, Leftism means anti-Imperialism. A genuine anti-imperialist is one who believes in undiluted independence (not Mahatma Gandhi's substance of independence) as the political objective and in uncompromising national struggle as the means for attaining it. After the attainment of political independence Leftism will mean Socialism and the task before the people will then be the reconstruction of national life on a Socialist basis. Socialism or Socialist reconstruction before achieving our political emancipation is altogether premature.

Genuine anti-imperialists, i.e. Leftists have always to fight on two fronts. So also in India, they have to fight on one side, foreign Imperialism and its Indian allies, and on the other, our milk-and-water nationalists, the Rightists, who are prepared for a deal with Imperialism. Genuine anti-Imperialists should therefore anticipate persecution not only at the hands of the known agents of alien Imperialism but also at the hands of their Rightist friends—and at times it may be difficult to say which persecution is more severe and trying. In the case of present-day India, the Rightists will stoop to any degree of ruthlessness in their persecution of the Leftists, because they have had a taste of power and are determined to monopolise it for themselves in future by rooting out all opposition.

To carry on a struggle on two fronts simultaneously and to face the above two-fold persecution is not an easy affair. There are people who may stand up to one type of persecution at a time, but not to both. There are others who can stomach persecution at the hands of an alien Government, but who quail when it comes to a question of fighting their Rightist friends. But if we are genuine anti-Imperialists and want to function as such, we must muster courage to fight on a double-front and face all the persecution that may come our way.

In India we often come across people who pose as Leftists and talk big things, including Socialism—but who manage to shirk a struggle when they are confronted with it and spin out ingenious arguments for buttressing themselves. Thus we see pseudo-Leftists who through sheer cowardice avoid a conflict with Imperialism and argue in self-defence that Mr Winston Churchill (whom we know to be the arch-Imperialist) is the greatest revolutionary going. It has become a fashion with these pseudo-Leftists to call the British Government a revolutionary force because it is fighting the Nazis and Fascists. But they conveniently forget the imperialist character of Britain's war and also the fact that the greatest revolutionary force in the world, the Soviet Union, has entered into a solemn pact with the Nazi Government.

Those who are prepared to face Imperialism but shrink from a clash with the Rightists, take shelter under a different argument. They hide their weakness under the plea of unity. But this is a specious plea which often results in self-deception. One should always distinguish between unity and unity—between the unity of action and the unity of inaction. And one should never forget that to talk of unity between those who are genuine anti-imperialists and those who are not—is mere moonshine. If unity under all circumstances is an end in itself, then why not establish unity between Congressmen and those who are outside the Congress or are against it? The argument of unity should not be carried beyond a certain point. Unity is certainly desirable, but only when there is agreement in principle and in policy. Unity at the sacrifice of one's principles or convictions is worthless and leads to inaction, while real unity is always a source of strength and stimulates activity. To avoid a clash with the Rightists by putting forward the plea of unity is nothing but weakness and cowardice.

In the light of these observations it should be easy to decide who are, and who are not, genuine Leftists and as to whether the Forward Bloc has proved by its action and conduct to be a genuine Leftist organisation. The question now is as to how Left-consolidation will ultimately be brought about. We have seen that three possible methods for achieving Left-consolidation have all failed. We also know that different individuals and parties have claimed to be Leftist. How then will the Left Movement develop in future?

The answer to this question is that the logic of history will determine who are the genuine Leftists. History will separate the chaff from the grain—the pseudo-Leftists from the genuine Leftists. When this elimination takes place, all the genuine Leftists will come together and fusion will take place. By this natural or historical process, Left-consolidation will be achieved. For this purpose, the acid-test of a fight on a double front is essential. Those who pass the test will be the genuine Leftists and they will all coalesce in time.

Since the Indians are a living nation, their political movement cannot die. And since stagnation has overtaken the Rightists, the logic of history demands a big Left Movement so that progress may continue. Conflict is bound to follow, but only for a time. Ultimately, Leftism will establish its supremacy over the entire political Movement of the land.

Since its inception, the Forward Bloc has been functioning as the spearhead of the Left Movement in India. Through its instrumentality, the Left forces have been gaining ground everyday and along with its ally, the Kishan Sabha, it will be largely responsible for bringing about Left-consolidation in future. By waging a fearless fight on a double-front and by welcoming simultaneous persecution at the hands of alien Imperialism and of the Indian Rightists it has established its claim to be a genuine Leftist organisation. It has therefore succeeded where other parties have failed.

The Forward Bloc is to the Left Movement what the Gandhiites are to the Right Movement. Philosophically speaking, the former may be regarded as the 'anti-thesis' of the latter. Though the Forward Bloc has always desired to work in close co-operation with the Gandhiites on the anti-imperialist front, the differences between the two are deep and fundamental. Gandhiism envisages an ultimate compromise with Imperialism for Gandhian Satyagraha (or Civil Disobedience) must end in a compromise. But Forward Bloc will have no truck with Imperialism. Socially, Gandhiism is intimately linked up with the 'haves'—the vested interests. As the 'have-nots' are becoming class-conscious, as is inevitable, the breach between them and the Gandhiites is widening. One therefore finds that unlike what was the position twenty years ago, today Gandhiism does not appeal to large masses of the peasantry and factory workers, nor does it appeal to middle class youths and students, the vast majority of whom sympathise with the poverty-stricken masses. With regard to the future, Gandhian ideas of post-struggle reconstruction, which are partly medieval and partly anti-socialist, are contrary to those of the Forward Bloc which has a thoroughly modern outlook and stands for Socialist Reconstruction.

Since its inauguration in May 1939, the Forward Bloc has developed in its ideology and programme—and naturally too—but there has been no change in fundamentals, except that at the Second All-India Conference held at Nagpur in June 1940, it was declared to be a party. Today, as it did yesterday, it stands for uncompromising national struggle for the attainment of Independence, and for the post struggle period, it stands for socialist reconstruction.

It would not be irrelevant to ask as to what the Forward Bloc has achieved so far and what potentiality it has for the future. Without indulging in exaggeration or in self-praise, we may make the following claim:

(1) It has saved the Congress from stagnation and death at the hands of the Rightists by building up a Leftist force. It has thereby fulfilled its historical role to a large extent.

(2) It has served to stem the drift towards Constitutionalism, to create a new revolutionary mentality among the people and to bring the Congress back to the path of struggle, however inadequately. Today nobody will gainsay the fact that but for the Anti-compromise Conference held at Ramgarh in March 1940, the Forward Bloc propaganda preceding it and the activities of the Bloc following it—Mahatma Gandhi would not have felt obliged to start the campaign of individual Civil Disobedience.

(3) The analysis and the forecast of the War made by the Forward Bloc have been proved to be correct.

(4) The propaganda and activities of the Forward Bloc have been responsible for inducing the Congress and Mahatma Gandhi to give the go-by to the original stand of the latter in September 1939, with reference to the War and to return to the war-policy advocated by the Congress from 1927 to 1938.

(5) In building up the Left Movement, the Forward Bloc has clarified the issues which separate the Left from the Right and has stimulated the intellectual and ideological progress of the Congress.

(6) The Forward Bloc has been functioning as a watchdog for warning the Congress and the country against any back-sliding on the part of any individual or party—particularly with reference to the major issues of the war-crisis and national struggle.

With reference to the future it may be confidently asserted:

(1) That the Forward Bloc will in the fullness of time succeed in

establishing Leftist ascendancy in the Congress so that the future progress of the latter may continue unhampered.

(2) It will prove to be the party of the future—the party that will give the proper lead in bringing the national movement to its fruition and will thereafter undertake the task of national reconstruction. Having sprung from the soil of India as a product of historical necessity and having at the same time the capacity to assimilate what is healthy and beneficial in the environment and in the world outside, it will be able to fulfil the dual role of conducting the National Struggle to its cherished goal and of building up a new India on the principles of liberty, equality and social justice.

(3) It will, by fulfilling its proper role, restore India to her proper and legitimate place in the comity of free nations.

(4) It will thereby enable India to play her historical role so that human progress may be taken a few stages beyond the point it has so far reached.

The ideas that are now uppermost in the minds of the Forward Bloc at the present time may be summarised as follows:

The Forward Bloc stands for:

(1) Complete National Independence and uncompromising anti-imperialist struggle for attaining it.

(2) A thoroughly modern and Socialist State.

(3) Scientific large-scale production for the economic regeneration of the country.

(4) Social ownership and control of both production and distribution.

(5) Freedom for the individual in the matter of religious worship.

(6) Equal rights for every individual.

(7) Linguistic and cultural autonomy for all sections of the Indian Community.

(8) Application of the principles of equality and social justice in building up the New Order in Free India.

The Forward Bloc is a revolutionary and dynamic organisation. As such it does not swear by copy-book maxims or by text-books of Politics or Economics. It is anxious to assimilate all the knowledge that the outside world can give and to profit by the experience of other progressive nations. It regards progress or evolution as an eternal process to which India also has a contribution to make.

Regarding the future career of the Forward Bloc we may confidently say that if it is the product of historical necessity, it will not die. If it has a philosophical justification, it will surely endure. And if it serves the cause of India, of humanity and of human progress, it will live and grow and no power on earth will ever destroy it.

Forward, therefore, and ever forward, my countrymen!

3

Plan of Indian Revolution

REPORT OF AN INTERVIEW[1]

Kabul 2nd April 1941
Sub: Subhas Chandra Bose—His Proposals about India
In continuation of my telegram n.124 I herewith give you in detail Bose's programme about India

As first step he thinks it would be convenient to constitute in Europe a 'Government of Free India' with a name to be decided upon; something on the lines of the various free governments that have been constituted in London.

Italy, Germany and Japan should promise, recognise and guarantee the independence and the integrity of India to the said government.

With such promise in hand the Government of Free India would begin a special radio campaign of its own on two basic subjects:

(1) The victory of the Axis is sure.
(2) There is nothing to hope for from England: in this moment of extreme danger for her, she still denies us an assurance for the status of 'Dominion' while the Axis powers guarantee us complete freedom and independence.

At the same time along with this propaganda campaign the Government of Free India would actively promote revolution in India as its contribution to the common fight against England: for this, naturally it would require help which should be given by the Axis powers in the form of a loan which India, once free, would pay back.

---

[1] This is a condensed version of a report made by Mr Alberto Quaroni, Italian Minister in Kabul, to his Government in Rome on his interview with Netaji in Kabul in March 1941. The meeting took place at the Italian Legation in Kabul during Netaji's secret sojourn in Afghanistan after his escape from India.—Eds.

According to Bose, India is morally ripe for the revolution, what is lacking is the courage to take the first step: the great obstacles to action are on one side the lack of faith in their own capabilities and on the other the blind persuasion of British excessive power. He says that if 50,000 men, Italian, German, or Japanese could reach the frontiers of India, the Indian army would desert, the masses would uprise and the end of English domination could be achieved in a very short time.

The evolution of the Indian public opinion—according to Bose—is deep in another sense also: till the beginning of the war a great part of the Indian political world was sincerely convinced that Italy, Germany and Japan were the enemies of humanity: after the start of the conflict and the fall of their hopes based on English politics, many Indians have started realising that they have been played low by England on this point.

As already mentioned—and on this point I cannot but agree with him—Bose is of the opinion that the main obstacle to the possibilities of a revolution in India is the great fear of England and, more than the fear, the belief that England with her strength and her luck will eventually overcome even this crisis: our recent defeats in Africa and in Greece plus the American attitude have contributed much to confirm this opinion also of those who last summer had begun doubting. I have said that this is correct; it is a state of mind that I see everyday in front of me in Afghanistan, where one has a more restricted view of international happenings than in India; the defeat of England is wanted and desired but there is fear to believe it.

The basic problem is therefore, according to Bose, to convince the Indians with facts and with propaganda that England can be beaten and shall be beaten ; once this is achieved one has already covered 70 per cent of the road.

Bose states that in the Indian political life today he is the person whose words carry most weight in foreign politics. He says that at the Tripuri meeting in which he invited the Congress to formulate a definite programme of action, I prophesied that the European war would start within six months. At the time I said that with a polemic aim only—he tells me—but chance wanted that the war did actually break out exactly within the six months, thereby I have risen to fame of being a person who can see more clearly than anybody else the international events: that is why, says he, the day I can say over the wireless 'Friends of India,

I have come to Europe, I have studied the situation and I am convinced that the Axis Powers will win, there will be more belief in my words than in those of anybody else.'

Incidentally he has told me that before broadcasting on the radio he must be convinced himself.

He will ask for the opportunity to organise in Italy or in Germany or maybe in both countries a special radio programme of the Free India.

He also proposes, in agreement with you, to keep in touch with India through the Kabul's central (see my report of even date) and to transmit to India this way the necessary means and instructions as and when required.

He would like also to intensify internal propaganda for desertion from the army, not sporadic desertion but mass desertion of entire divisions, and this would naturally be a very good thing. I asked him what are the possibilities in the field of terrorism. He replied that the terroristic organisation of Bengal and other similar ones in different parts of India still exist, but he is not much convinced of the usefulness of terrorism. He had never considered changing the activities of said organisations from individual efforts to organised sabotage: he liked the idea very much and through his secretary has sent instructions to the chief of the organisation in Bengal to work on this new way, who, according to what he says, is in close touch with him. I have told him that in Berlin and in Rome he could get all the practical advice on the mode of action and also all the technical means for action. It is clear that if large scale sabotage could be organised at a moment when India plays such an important part in the war supplies of the British army in the middle east, it would be a thing of no mean importance.

Bose is the type that we all know from his works and his actions, intelligent, able, full of passion and without doubt the most realistic, maybe the only realist, among the Indian nationalist leaders.

India is a problem too vast and complex to be able to express an opinion with full sense of responsibility from here in Kabul—an opinion on the practical feasibility of what Bose proposes to do.

As I have already informed you, what he says about the Indian situation tallies with what one can be made out of the very censored Indian Press; which is a sign that his statements do not sin of optimism and this is a thing in his favour.

My impression of the Indian situation from what I could gather from the different sources at my disposal, and lastly from my encounters with Bose, is the following:

If in June 1940, that is at the time when the defeat of England seemed certain, we had a ready organisation like the one Bose proposes now, it could have been attempted to liberate India, and it might have been possible.

Politically and militarily India is the corner-stone of the British Empire.

Last year's chance is gone, but a similar one could come this year also: one should be ready to take full advantage of it.

To put up this organisation money will be required, probably not little of it.

In the past, we have spent big sums of money, for instance on Press propaganda in the two Americas, with the results that we can see today: here one can work on a much more solid terrain. If what is being attempted should work out even in part, probably several months of war, human lives, millions worth of materials will be saved.

Our enemies, in all their wars, the present one included, have always largely used the 'revolution' weapon with success ; why should we not learn from our enemies?

Two things are necessary to make revolutions: men and money. We do not have the men to start a revolution in India, but luck has put them in our hands ; no matter how difficult Germany's and our monetary situation is, the money that this movement requires is certainly not lacking.

It is only a question of valuing the pros and cons and to decide on the risk.

A. Quaroni

4

Secret Memorandum to the German Government

BERLIN, 9 APRIL 1941

Plan for Cooperation Between the Axis Powers and India

As in the World War of 1914–18, so also in the present war, Great Britain has been endeavouring to exploit India for her war purposes. Since the war began, Great Britain has not relaxed her political and economic grip over India in spite of the manifold defeats she has suffered at the hands of Germany. To us in India, it is therefore crystal clear that as the British Empire collapses increasingly, Great Britain will try to hold on to India more and more and she will do so till the very last. It is also clear from British policy in India at the present time that if the British Empire somehow survives this war, Great Britain will endeavour to recover her strength by exploiting the rich resources of India so that she may be able to challenge the 'New Order' after some years.

India is naturally interested in seeing Great Britain completely vanquished in this war and the British Empire completely broken up, so that India may attain her national independence. The British Empire constitutes the greatest obstacle not only in the path of India's freedom but also in the path of human progress.

Since the attitude of the Indian people is intensely hostile to the British in the present war, it is possible for them to materially assist in bringing about the overthrow of Great Britain. India's cooperation could be secured if the Indian people are assured that an Axis victory will mean for them a free India.

In order to establish full cooperation between the Axis Powers and India for the achievement of the common objectives of defeating Great Britain, the following plan is being proposed: It will entail work in

Europe, in Afghanistan, in the Independent Tribal Territory lying between Afghanistan and India and last but not least in India.

I. Work in Europe

(1) A 'Free Indian Government' should be set up in Europe and preferably in Berlin.
(2 A treaty should be entered into between the Axis Powers and the free Indian Government providing, inter alia, for India's independence in the event of an Axis victory, special facilities for the Axis Powers in India when an independent government is set up there, etc.
(3) Legations of the Free Indian Government should be established in friendly countries wherever possible.
(N.B. The above measures will convince the Indian people that their independence has been guaranteed by the Axis Powers in the event of an Axis victory and that the status of independence is being recognised already in actual practice.)
(4) Propaganda, particularly through the radio, should then be started, calling upon the Indian people to assert their independence and to rise in revolt against the British authorities. Broadcasting will be done in the name of the Free Indian Radio Station.
(5) Arrangements should be made to send necessary help to India through Afghanistan for helping the revolution.

The help that India will require is being mentioned below.

II. Work in Afghanistan (Kabul)

(1) A centre will have to be established in Kabul for maintaining communications between Europe on the one hand and India on the other. The existing legations may be so enlarged as to be able to undertake this work or new committees may be set up specially for this purpose.
(2) The centre should have necessary equipment, like cars, lorries, special messengers, etc., for maintaining communications between Europe and India.

III. Work in the Tribal Territory

(1) Our agents are already working in the independent Tribal Territory lying between Afghanistan and India. Their efforts will have to be coordinated and an attack on British military centres will have to be planned on a large scale. The isolated attack now being carried out by such anti-British elements as the Fakir of Ipi will have to fit into this larger plan.

(2) Some military advisers from Europe will have to be sent to the Tribal Territory.

(3) A strong propaganda centre will have to be installed in the Tribal Territory and necessary printing equipment will have to be arranged for.

(4) A radio transmitting station will have to be set up in the Tribal Territory.

(5) Agents from the Tribal Territory will have to be appointed for procuring military intelligence from the Frontier Province of India, i.e. the province adjoining the Tribal Territory.

IV. Work in India

(1) Broadcasting for India will have to be done on a large scale. It will have to be done first from stations in Europe, and, later on, from stations in the Tribal Territory as well.

(2) The printing centre in the Tribal Territory will also be in charge of propaganda in India.

(3) Our agents and members of our party in the different provinces in India will be instructed to give the maximum trouble possible to the British authorities in India. Their work will consist of:

   (A) Intensive propaganda calling upon the Indian people not to give one soldier or one rupee to the British Government.

   (B) Propaganda calling upon the civilian population to defy the civil authorities by refusing to pay taxes, refusing to obey the orders and the laws of the British Government etc.

   (C) Secret work among the Indian section of the Army in order to induce them to rise in revolt.

   (D) Organising strikes in factories which work for helping Great Britain in her war efforts.

(E) Carrying out sabotage of strategic railway bridges, factories, etc. (Necessary material for this work will have to be sent to India).

(F) Organising revolts among the civil population in the different parts of the country as a stepping-stone to a general mass revolution.

V. QUESTION OF FINANCES

Necessary finances for the above work will have to be provided by the Axis Powers. This will be in the form of a loan to the Free Indian Government established in Europe. At the end of the War, when an independent Government is set up in India, the loan will be repaid in full.

For the expenditure in Europe, payment will naturally have to be made in Marks. For the expenditure in Afghanistan, Marks can be converted into 'Afghanis'. For the expenditure in India, 'Afghanis' can be converted into Rupees, though it is becoming somewhat difficult now. But perhaps Ten Rupee notes could be printed in Europe and sent to India via Afghanistan.

Memorandum: Explanatory Note

I. Lesson of the World War of 1914–18
II. Future of the British Empire as considered by us
III. The importance of India in the British Empire
IV. Some aspects of British diplomacy in the present war
V. The attitude of the Indian people in the present war as compared with their attitude in the world war of 1914–18
VI. The military position in India today
VII. The importance for India of Japanese foreign policy in the Far East

I. LESSON OF THE WORLD WAR OF 1914–18

The World War of 1914–18 had several lessons for humanity, but for the purpose of this note, I shall refer to only one. At the conclusion of that war, when the time came to remake the map of Europe, the Allied

Powers—and Great Britain and France in particular—wanted to smash the Central Powers in such a manner that they would not be able to raise their heads again. The iniquities of the Treaty of Versailles were manifold, but Great Britain and France did not nevertheless succeed in disturbing the fundamental integrity and homogeneity of the German Reich. On the other hand, the two Empires, Austro-Hungarian and Ottoman, were completely broken up and today we see clearly what the result of that break-up has been. But for the German Reich, there would have been no power in Europe at the present time to challenge the Anglo-French combination.

It is clear from the events of the last few years and particularly from the events of the last twelve months, that the one outstanding obstacle in the path of building up a new Europe and a new world is the heterogeneous British Empire. And even if Great Britain is defeated in the present war, she will still remain the implacable foe of progress and evolution. Consequently, if the integrity of the British Empire is left untouched at the end of the war, it will be able to recover after a few years and then challenge the New Order. If the New Order is to last, the British Empire will have to be put out of action once for all and, to that end, it will have to be broken up completely.

The potential resources of the British Empire are incalculable and India is still the jewel of that Empire. If a defeated Great Britain is given time and opportunity to develop these resources, she will be in position to fight again and perhaps more effectively. From the policy and administration of the British Government in India since September 1939, it is clear that the more she has been collapsing in Europe, the more she has been trying to tighten her grip over India and to exploit the resources of that country for her selfish purpose. This effort will continue in future and we in India have no doubt in our minds that if the integrity of the British Empire is left untouched at the end of the present war, a defeated Great Britain will once again threaten the peace of the world after a decade or two.

It is for the Axis Powers to consider whether they should now treat Great Britain in the same manner in which she treated the Austro-Hungarian and Ottoman Empires in 1918–19. If Great Britain is to be paid back in her own coin, then the British Empire will have to be broken up completely and the countries that are now under the British yoke will have to be set free. It should be remembered in this connection that even if India alone is left with Great Britain and the other parts of the Empire are dismembered, Great Britain with the assistance of the potential resources of India, will be in a position to challenge the New Order after some years.

Future peace in Europe at the end of this war demands imperatively a New Order, not only in Europe and Africa, but throughout the world. And with this New Order, the question of India is inseparably connected.

II. Future of the British Empire as Considered by Us

Even before the present war began, we in India were definitely of opinion that the British Empire was decadent. This was not the result of a theoretical knowledge of the laws operating in the history of mankind, but was the conclusion we reached after an observation of indisputable facts. The Empire had given the British people untold wealth and immeasurable resources but it had also given them comfort and luxury, self-complacency and arrogance. Consequently, deterioration in character and morals followed. One aspect of this deterioration is bankruptcy in diplomacy and statesmanship. The British we find in India and in Great Britain today are not the British we would find fifty years ago.

While on the one hand the British people have been deteriorating during the last few decades, there has been a phenomenal awakening among the suppressed nations of the Empire and particularly in India. The process of deterioration is thus being expedited by the pressures coming from different parts of the British Empire, e.g. Ireland (Eire), South Africa, Palestine, India etc. owing to this national awakening everywhere.

It needed a war like the present one to expose to the world the fact that the mighty British Lion was not in reality as powerful as it appeared to be, but had feet of clay. The Empire owed its birth and continuance to military strength, including sea-power, and prestige. When internal deterioration set in and different parts of the Empire began to strive for their independence, other Western nations were making rapid progress in science, industry, methods of warfare etc. and Great Britain was not able to keep abreast of them. To a keen observer it was quite clear that the ultimate fate of the British Empire was doomed and it only needed an international clash to bring about its speedy down-fall. Till this clash took place in September 1939, the British Empire was, however, able to maintain its existence and keep up appearances through its past prestige. The series of overwhelming defeats which England has suffered in the different war-fronts since September 1939, have now not only exposed her actual military position, but also have shattered her prestige throughout the world including the dependencies and colonies of Great Britain. During the course of this note I shall show that with her prestige completely shattered and her actual military position so thoroughly exposed before the world, the British regime in India today is like a house of cards.

According to our view in India, when the collapse of the British Empire comes about, the following developments are likely to take place. Canada, Australia and New Zealand, will gravitate towards the United States of America. Ireland, South Africa, India, Palestine, Egypt, Iraq, etc. will throw off the British yoke and attain full-fledged independence. And the African colonies of England will be divided among the other powers. Great Britain will remain as the third class power in Europe, with no influence on the Continent.

It is within the reach of the Axis Powers to bring about the immediate collapse of the British Empire and its complete dismemberment. And it is possible for India to help in this task. It is hardly necessary to add that we in India want to see the complete dismemberment of this Empire, for we regard it as the greatest curse in modern history.

III. The Importance of India in the British Empire

India with her vast population and untold natural resources and incalculable potential wealth, is the jewel of the British Empire and it is the exploitation of India in the past which has made the British Empire what it is today. Nevertheless, it must be said that so far Great Britain has exploited only a fraction of the resources of India's men and materials. A policy of full exploitation would have entailed more education for the people and more industrialisation in the country and this the British Government has up till now hesitated to undertake. In the present war we have seen that the British Government has been able to exploit such parts of the Empire as Ireland, South Africa, etc. to the extent that she wanted to—and as the days roll by, she has been trying to exploit India more and more for her selfish purposes. There were some Indians who wrongly thought at one time that as the position of Great Britain became precarious in Europe, she would relax her hold over India and concede the demand of the Indian people for national independence. But quite the contrary has actually occurred. We now find that the attitude of the British Government towards India's demand for freedom has become more stiff since the war began. British industrialists and experts have, moreover, been sent out to India to exploit that country and even such pro-British Indian industrialists who are thoroughly efficient and competent and run such huge concerns as the Tata Iron and Steel Company of Jamshedpur, the Iron and Steel Works of Mysore, the Scindia Steam Navigation Company, etc. are not given any share in the new plan of economic exploitation. Therefore, if we look at British policy in India today there cannot be the slightest doubt that England is determined to reserve India for her own, exclusive exploitation and that the Indian people will not be allowed to have either their political freedom or liberty to develop their country industrially.

Consequently, it follows that if Great Britain can somehow avoid a break-up of the Empire in spite of being defeated in the present war, she will get breathing-time and by exploiting the vast resources of India, will try again to disturb the New Order which will be ushered in at the end of this war.

India's freedom will make it impossible for Great Britain to raise her head again. And India by striving for freedom now can materially assist in bringing about the overthrow of Great Britain.

IV. SOME ASPECTS OF BRITISH DIPLOMACY IN THE PRESENT WAR

It is one of the cardinal principles of British diplomacy to adopt a sanctimonious role when she is fighting in reality for her own selfish interests. We saw in the World War that Great Britain posed as the champion of smaller nations and we see it now again. At the present time, in order to show that she is the champion of smaller nations, she is giving asylum in a most liberal manner to refugees from Czechoslovakia, Poland, Norway, Holland, Belgium, France, etc. These refugees like Benes, Sikorsi, King of Norway, Queen of Holland, De Gaulle of France, etc. are allowed to set up their own Governments in London under the name of 'free' Governments. They are given the full diplomatic status of independent Governments by virtue of special legislation and most, if not all, of these 'Governments' are financed by the British. By this clever subterfuge Great Britain endeavours to show to the world that she is in reality the champion of smaller nations.

Why should not the Axis Powers adopt the same policy and pay England back in her own coin? There are so many nations that are under the yoke of Great Britain and have been striving to throw off that yoke. The representatives of these suppressed nations could very well form their 'free' Governments in the Axis countries in Europe; thereby they could counteract British propaganda on the one hand and on the other help the revolution in their respective countries. This could easily be done at least in the case of India.

V. THE ATTITUDE OF THE INDIAN PEOPLE IN THE PRESENT WAR AS COMPARED WITH THEIR ATTITUDE IN THE WAR OF 1914–18

In the World War the propaganda of the British Government in India was very successful and very little of German propaganda reached that country. Consequently, though the real desire of the people was that England should be defeated in the war, the impression was nevertheless created that the Allied Powers were very strong and would undoubtedly win. Under this impression many of the older leaders in India were persuaded to give their moral support to Great Britain in her war efforts. During that war, Great Britain was able to recruit one and half million soldiers in India and also to raise large sums of money as a free gift from India for the prosecution of the war. On the present occasion, the situation is quite the reverse of what it was in 1914–18. British propaganda in India has been a failure in spite of its best efforts and nobody now imagines that Great Britain can be victorious this time. Anti-War propaganda has been carried on systematically by the Indian National Congress for several years, with the result that there is no sympathy for the British Government among the Indian people. Moreover, German propaganda through the radio is now able to reach India. The cumulative effect of all these factors has been that this time it took the British Government 15 months to recruit one hundred thousand soldiers in a poverty-stricken country like India in spite of all kinds of monetary temptation. And even these men will not be loyal to the British Government! The monetary help which Britain has received from India this time is a meagre fraction of what she got in 1914–18. And even this amount has been subscribed chiefly by the British industrialists in India and the Maharajas. The people's contribution has been practically nothing. During the period from September 1939 to June 1940, I delivered at least one thousand lectures from one end of the country to the other, at which I put the question straight to the people as to whether they would like to see Great Britain defeated this time. And at every meeting they enthusiastically declared that they would like to see the Empire overthrown, so that India could be free.

VI. The Military Position in India Today

The attitude of the Indian people which was hostile to Great Britain at the beginning of the war has been greatly embittered as a result of the imprisonment of most of the leaders and thousands of their followers in every province in India. As there is no possibility of any change in Britain's policy in India while the war lasts, it is certain that the hatred of the people towards British domination will become deeper and deeper as the days roll by. England is thus holding India by the sword at the present time. But even from the military point of view the British position is not as strong as it appears from the outside and only a strong blow is needed to make the house of cards topple down in India.

The full strength of the Army in India, including auxiliaries like the armed police and territorials is approximately 250,000. Since the beginning of the war about 100,000 men were sent out on service abroad, i.e. to the Near East, Middle East and Far East. This deficiency was recouped by an additional recruitment of 100,000 which it took the British Government 15 months to secure. It is now the plan of the Government to recruit an additional force of 500,000 for service during war-time, but it is extremely doubtful if the Government will be able to raise even a part of this force.

Out of this total figure of 250,000 the British troops including auxiliaries, number 70,000. The Indian troops number about 1,80,000 but they are officered by the British. There is only a small percentage of Indian Officers for the Indian soldiers.

The Indian army is equipped with modern equipment like aeroplanes, tanks, armoured cars, mechanised transport, heavy artillery, etc. though their number is small. They have so far proved to be enough for holding the country in subjugation, but they are most inadequate for fighting a modern army possessing modern equipment.

Rifles, small ammunition and explosives are now being manufactured in India, but other modern equipment like aeroplanes, tanks, armoured cars, motor cars, lorries, heavy artillery, etc. are all imported. During the last few months the British authorities have been constructing large underground shelters on the hillside near the North Western Frontier of India for storing bombs, ammunition, etc.

The British section of the Army in India having a maximum strength of 70,000 is the only loyal force in India on whom the British Government can fully depend. The Indian section of the army has many anti-British elements and perhaps the only group that will be loyal to the British is composed of the Punjabi Muslims. The Punjabi Sikhs—the best fighters in the Indian Army—are the most anti-British at the present time. Since the war began, many regiments of Punjabi Sikhs have mutinied and they have been court-martialled. I know this from personal experience, because those who were not shot, were sentenced to long terms of imprisonment and then they were transported to the Andaman Islands; they passed through the same jail in which I was incarcerated from July to December 1940, viz. the Presidency Jail in Calcutta.

As already stated above, British prestige in India is shattered as a result of the many defeats which the British have suffered in the present war. As a matter of fact, after the fall of France in June 1940, the Indian Army was in a mood in which there was utter lack of confidence in British military strength. That was the proper psychological moment for a revolution, but it was not availed of by the Indian people. A similar opportunity will come again when Britain receives another severe blow at the hands of the Axis Powers.

When the opportunity comes again and if it is properly utilised revolts can be brought about in the Indian section of the Army, in spite of the British personnel of the officers.

In that revolutionary crisis, the British Government will have only the British soldiers to fall back on. If at that juncture, some military help is available from abroad (i.e. a small force of 50,000 men with modern equipment) British power in India can be completely wiped out.

VII. THE IMPORTANCE FOR INDIA OF JAPANESE FOREIGN POLICY IN THE FAR EAST

The overthrow of British power in India can, in its last stages, be materially assisted by Japanese foreign policy in the Far East. If Japan decides on expansion southwards it will lead to an open clash with Great Britain. If war then breaks out, it appears more than certain that the East Indies and Far Eastern squadrons of the British Navy will, under the present circumstances, be no match for the Japanese Navy. And even if America comes to the rescue of the British Navy, a Japanese victory could still be hoped for. A defeat of the British Navy in the Far East including the smashing up of the Singapore base, will automatically weaken British military strength and prestige in India. India is, therefore, intensely interested in the developments in the Far East. And since Japanese expansion southwards necessitates a prior agreement between the Soviets and Japan, India is greatly interested in a pact which will, on the one hand, expedite a settlement of the China Affair and will, on the other, enable Japan to move more freely and confidently towards the South.

5

Supplementary Memorandum to the German Government

BERLIN, 3 MAY 1941

The recent victories of Germany in North Africa, Yugoslavia and Greece have created a profound impression in all Oriental countries, particularly in India, and in the countries of the Near East like Egypt, Palestine and Iraq. British prestige in all these countries has been shattered and it is well known that Great Britain has up till now dominated Oriental countries largely because of her prestige as a world power. Simultaneously with Britain's loss of prestige, several Oriental countries have begun to assert themselves in opposition to Great Britain.

I. This opposition has been openly manifested in Iraq.
II. From India are coming daily reports of unrest in several important centres.
III. In Egypt, after a long silence, the Wafd Party has raised its voice demanding that the Egyptian people should not participate in Britain's war against Germany.
IV. In other Arab countries like Palestine, there is a strong undercurrent of unrest against Britain which can be worked up into an open revolt.

At this psychological moment, the Axis Powers can capture the imagination of the entire Orient by an open declaration of policy with regard to the Orient and, in particular, with regard to India and the Arab countries. The latter countries hate Britain because she is an Imperialist power and they can be drawn into the Axis orbit if they are convinced that the Axis Powers will champion their emancipation from the British yoke. Even in those countries where there was a large measure of pro-Soviet feeling before the beginning of the present war (as in India), it is now realised that it is the Axis Powers alone (and not the

Soviet) that can render practical help to them in their struggle for emancipation from British domination.

I therefore request

I. that an early pronouncement be made regarding the freedom of India and of the Arab countries.
II. that the work of organising revolts against Great Britain in these countries be commenced as soon as possible, so that the present favourable atmosphere in these countries may be properly utilised.
III. that the Axis Powers do now concentrate on attacking the heart of the British Empire, that is, British rule in India.
IV. that in order to facilitate the attack on British rule in India, steps be taken to upset the present pro-British Government in Afghanistan.
V. that steps be taken to render military aid to Iraq against Great Britain, should that become necessary in future.

If this proposal is accepted and the work suggested is undertaken by the Axis Powers, then Germany will have the following advantages:

(A) There will be a long chain of friendly pro-German countries beginning from North Africa on the one side and right up to Japan in the Far East.
(B) If a conflict between Germany on the one hand and Soviet Russia or Turkey on the other, proves to be unavoidable in future, then Germany will have the sympathy of all the Oriental countries.

But if in the meantime a conflict with Turkey or the Soviet breaks out before the above proposal is given effect to, then Germany will probably lose the sympathy of the Oriental countries which she has gained because of her fight against British Imperialism.

For the success of the task of exterminating British power and influence from the countries of the Near and Middle East, it is desirable that the status quo between Germany and Soviet Russia should be maintained.

In order to strike at British power in India, it is necessary to have some channel of communication between Germany on the one side and Afghanistan and India on the other. There are four alternative routes which appear possible and it is for the experts (military and political) to decide which routes they would prefer as being the most practicable:

Route I. Germany, Russia, Afghanistan, India
Route II. Balkans, Turkey, (Syria?) Iraq, Persian Gulf and India
Route III. Balkans, Turkey, (Syria and Iraq?), Iran, Afghanistan and India.
Route IV. Libya, Egypt, Suez Canal and India.

From the point of view of convenience, Route I appears to be the most desirable.

In any case, the indirect help of Soviet Russia or of Turkey is necessary for opening up a channel of communication between Germany on the one side and Afghanistan and India on the other.

When a channel of communication is once made, it will become easy for Germany to strike at British power and influence in Afghanistan and India. Then will come the end of the British Empire.

3.5.41   SUBHAS CHANDRA BOSE

N.B. After the above note was written, the Berlin radio and newspaper give the report that fighting between the British and the Irakies has taken place in Iraq. This will have a powerful reaction in all Oriental countries and particularly among the Arabs. The need of an immediate decision regarding the Oriental policy of Germany has thus become all the more urgent. I therefore request once more an immediate decision, so that the present psychological atmosphere may be fully utilised against Great Britain.

Enclosure: A cutting from 'B.Z.am Mittag' of 3.5.41

6

Secret Message to Comrades in India

MAY 1941[1]

Big events will happen soon in sphere of international politics which will help the overthrow of British Imperialism. Time is therefore ripe for widespread propaganda and activity against Britain throughout the world and particularly in Oriental countries. To this work Indians can contribute much but they must speak and act in the name of Free India. I am expecting from the Axis Powers within a fortnight an open declaration regarding Indian Independence. Immediately after this declaration I intend starting propaganda and activity, including radio propaganda, in name of Free India Movement. I expect the Axis declaration to say that the constitution of the Free Indian State will be decided by the Indian people themselves. My propaganda also will avoid party questions and simply appeal to the Indian people to fight for their liberty and take the help of all friendly powers. In my opinion the good results that will follow from my open propaganda in India will far outweigh the bad results, if any. If you have any serious objections to my starting open propaganda even after the Axis declaration regarding Indian Independence then please return to India, consult friends and come back to Kabul and report to me. It is particularly necessary to consult Sarat Bose in Calcutta on this point. If however you agree that I should start propaganda after the Axis Declaration then let me know at once.

Please let me know names of important men you met in India. Have you delivered to Sarat Bose the personal letters and the long article? Has the party published my statement on why I left India which I sent with you? Did you meet the Moulana at Adda Sahib and will he actively help us? When you go to India next time please arrange that emissaries

1 This secret message was sent by Netaji to Kabul in May 1941. Mr Quaroni, a diplomat in the Italian Legation there, gave it to Sarat Chandra Bose when they met in Paris in 1948.

are sent to our party members in Central and South India including Bombay so that they may be instructed to work in line with the rest of India.

It is absolutely necessary that Sardul Singh Cavesheer believes that you are acting as my agent. You can easily convince him through Calcutta friends or through Akbar Shah. Please request Sardul Singh to keep up friendly contacts with AHRAR PARTY and JAMIAT ULEMA and AKALI PARTY. In spite of our ideological difference we must have friendly relations with Akalis. We need Sardul Singh to represent the public activity of Forward Bloc. Sarat Bose will be able to influence him properly.

Please organise a Nepalese group to work among Gurkha troops in India and also to go to Nepal for secret activity there. Calcutta friends could supply reliable Nepalese from Darjeeling. New German Commercial Attache will reach Kabul within a fortnight and he will give advice regarding Nepal where he had made contacts.

Please ask Calcutta friends to send out emissaries to Burma to make contact with DOBAMA and other revolutionary parties there and bring back correct information for me regarding the political situation there and possibility of revolution.

Please organise military espionage not only in Frontier and Punjab but in all military centres in India. Information already collected should be brought to Kabul and preserved there in writing so that they may be used in future when necessary. Please collect detailed information regarding the composition of the troops in the frontier according to religion and province and whether infantry or cavalry or artillery, etc.

Have you enquired if suitable land for aerodrome is available in Tribal Territory? If not please do so at once. Please consider also how to bring petrol there and from where.

I intend having a centre in friendly Tribal Territory for special military training of Indians. Can you arrange necessary accommodation and good arrangements for this centre? Can you also arrange for some European military officers to stay there?

Have you attempted to organise a big ZIRGA (conference) of all anti-British Tribal leaders for organising an attack on the British on a large scale?

Please arrange a relay of trusted messengers between Kabul and Peshawar and between Peshawar and Calcutta who will constantly come and go with information and instructions. For the first few months you should come personally to Kabul once a month. Please arrange your substitute for liaison work in case you are suddenly arrested. Have you arranged centres in Kabul where friends from India can stay? Make such arrangements in Kabul that Europeans could be conveniently smuggled into the Tribal Territory from there. Arrange for car and lorry in Kabul for this purpose and also for other work in Kabul. We can begin sending help for India from June. I am trying for Radio Transmitter for Tribal Territory. We can also send propaganda leaflets and booklets. Please arrange for these and sabotage materials and other articles to be taken to India from Kabul.

Do you want cyclostyle or duplicator machines or small-printing presses for Tribal Territory or for India?

What arms do you want for Tribal Territory and for India? Have you enquired about quality and quantity of arms produced in factories in Tribal Territory which can be purchased by us?

Is radio propaganda from Berlin and Rome necessary in Pushtu language?

Please bring from India report regarding reaction of the Indian people and particularly Indian Muslims to the Anglo-Iraq war.

If you have absolutely reliable men please put some into the new army that the British are trying to raise in India so that they may work within the army. Special care and caution will be necessary in selecting such men.

Will Uttam Chand do any serious work for us in future?

Where is Sodhi now? Please keep him for work in Tribal Territory.

Before you leave Kabul please send a detailed report of your last visit to Tribal Territory and India.

Please bring for me reports of the National Planning Committee and its Sub-Committees. You will get them from Bombay office.

Please send a plan of the work you propose to do in India and the Tribal Territory for working up a revolution and also the timetable if possible. What help do you want from here for that work? If you cannot send me the plan now, please send it after consulting friends in India.

When you leave Kabul please visit Tribal Territory and important Indian centres and come back after one month.

Please take necessary money with you from Kabul but be economical in expenditure.

7

Draft of the Free India Declaration

'Mazzotta', May 1941[1]

In order to clarify its policy regarding India, the Government of Great Germany is making the following declaration:

'India, with an ancient culture and civilisation which she has preserved up to the present day, has always fascinated the imagination of the German people and, as is universally known, the cultural bonds between Germany and India have during a long period been close and intimate. It is consequently natural that Germany should follow with the deepest interest the struggle of the Indian people for their emancipation from the yoke of British Imperialism. Germany is now in a position to go further and declare that the right of the Indian people to the ownership of India and the unfettered control of Indian destinies is sovereign and indefensible. The usurpation of that right by a foreign people and Government neither has, nor can it ever extinguish that right. Germany therefore recognises the inalienable right of the Indian people to have full and complete independence, to enjoy the fruits of their toil and have all the necessities of life, so that they may have full opportunities of growth. She assures the Indian people that the New Order which she is out to establish in the world will mean for them a free and independent India. Germany feels confident that when the Indian people are liberated from the political domination and the economic exploitation of British Imperialism and become masters of their own destiny, they will bring about the all-round regeneration of their national life and thereby contribute to the common good of mankind.

It will, of course, be for the Indian people to decide what form of Government they should have, when they are free. It will also be their

---

[1] Subhas Chandra Bose wrote this draft of a Declaration guaranteeing the freedom of India, probably in the second half of May 1941. Source: AA-A/Kult. R., vol. 8, England (German Foreign Office).

task to determine how the national constitution should be framed, whether by a Constituent Assembly or by the leaders of the people or by some other machinery. But it is only natural that Germany, in keeping with her own traditions, would like to see in India a united nation, in which every individual is guaranteed food, work, necessities of life and equal opportunities of growth, regardless of religion, class or any other consideration. Germany conveys its sincerest good wishes to the Indian people in their struggle for freedom and declares that she is prepared to render them such assistance as lies in her power, so that the goal of liberty may be reached without delay. She now waits for the day when independent India will have her own national Government.

Germany will gladly recognise that Government and establish friendly relations with it.'

8

A Gloomy Scenario

Letter to Dr Woermann of the German Foreign Office, 5 July 1941

Dear Dr Woermann,

I am glad to have your letter of the 24th June which reached me on the 28th ultimo and I thank you for the contents thereof.

I met Count Ciano after his return from Venice, as desired by him. The talk was not encouraging for me and soon after that, the war in the East broke out. The prospect for the realisation of my plans looked gloomy in the altered circumstances and I was thinking that an early return to Berlin would not be of much use, till the situation in the East was clarified. I was therefore happy to receive your letter.

I have informed the Foreign Office that I intend to leave soon and I have arranged to start for Vienna on Tuesday the 8th inst. I shall be stopping at Grand Hotel in Vienna for a few days and shall be in Berlin on Monday, the 14th inst., at the latest. If you so desire, I could cut short my stay in Vienna and proceed straight to Berlin. If so, kindly send me a message at the Grand Hotel or the Konaorzialrat Otto Faltis. Wien I. Tuchiauben 7a/19, Telephone: U 21-1-80.

The public reaction in my country to the new situation in the East is unfavourable towards your Government. However, I am following the situation as closely as I can and I shall discuss the whole matter with you as soon as I arrive.

With kind regards,

Yours sincerely,

O. Mazzotta

9

The Russo-German War and Indian Struggle

REPORT OF A CONVERSATION WITH THE
GERMAN FOREIGN OFFICE, 17 JULY 1941[1]

Mr Bose came to meet me today after his return.

I first informed him about the tasks assigned to the Secretary of State Keppler. After his visit with me, Mr Bose called on Mr Keppler.

Bose at first spoke at length about the reactions of the Russo-German War on public opinion in India. The Soviet Union had been popular in India, especially among the intellectuals from whom the leaders are drawn. It is believed in India that the Soviet Union is an anti-imperialist power and would therefore be India's ally against England. The Russo-German Pact of 1939 was an event of the highest significance for India. It made it possible for the intellectuals, who anyway were drawn to National Socialism, to look upon Germany and Italy as forces which would bring about the end of British rule in India in friendship with the Soviet Union, although British propaganda had succeeded in keeping alive sentiments of enmity towards the Axis powers in most parts of India. In the German-Russian War, the sympathies of the Indian people were very clearly with Russia because the Indian people felt definitely that Germany was the aggressor and was for India, and without complete German victory over Russia, it would be difficult to change public opinion in India in this respect.

At the same time Bose expects—as is confirmed by reports received from London—that England is now going to introduce reforms in India,

[1] Netaji was in Rome when the Russo-German War broke out. He immediately communicated his reactions to this major turn in world affairs *vis-à-vis* the Indian struggle for independence to the German Foreign Office. On his return to Berlin, he had a discussion with Herr Woermann, a Secretary of State at the German Foreign Office. This is a translation of the report submitted by Herr Woermann to the German Government on his interview with Netaji.

which will encourage that section of the Indian public that is always in favour of compromise, to continue to stake their cards on the English; simultaneously the threat of a German attack on India will be presented to the public not as one intended to liberate the Indian people but to substitute British rule by German rule.

Bose expects that India will become, more than before, a centre of British military expansion. He considers it very probable that England will proceed, not across Afghanistan, but via Iran in order, first, to take possession of the oilfields and then, to get close to the Soviet Union in the region of the Caucasus.

It was clear from his statements that Bose is, being far from Berlin, strongly influenced by the Soviet thesis on the question of the origin of the German-Russian conflict; it will therefore be one of our first tasks to put him right in this respect.

I told Bose that we remain firm in our intention regarding a proclamation for a free India; we have of course to choose a suitable time for it.

Here Mr Bose became very emphatic and asked that the Reich Foreign Minister be requested to issue this proclamation as speedily as possible. Each day that passed meant an advantage to England because of the reforms that she intended to introduce in India. On the other hand, he saw no reason to postpone this proclamation. He however agreed that the date had to be fixed with due consideration of the entire situation.

During this short interview I went thoroughly into the other current questions, especially the proposed Free India Centre. It was however obvious that these questions were of minor interest to Bose as long as he was not sure about the declaration on a Free India.

I request attention to the report of the German Embassy in Rome dated July 13th and the reports of the Italian Foreign Office concerning Bose's discussions in Rome. I consider the proposal No.4 where it is suggested that Bose be kept in a neutral country in reserve until a more convenient time in future, to be inadvisable.

Submitted to the Reich Foreign Minister.

Suggestions for further discussion regarding relevant questions are being prepared by the Secretary of State Keppler and me.

WOERMANN

10

The Approach of an Enemy

LETTER TO GERMAN FOREIGN MINISTER
VON RIBBENTROP, 15 AUGUST 1941

Your Excellency,

I feel constrained to take the liberty of addressing Your Excellency because the situation in India today is extremely serious.

I have been here since the beginning of April and my proposals were placed before Your Excellency soon after my arrival.

The situation in my country was then exceedingly favourable for the success of my proposals. Unfortunately, no decision was arrived at by the German Government and since then, the situation in India has worsened considerably.

The outbreak of the war with Soviet Russia has been made to appear to India as an act of aggression and Soviet-British-American propaganda has made the fullest use of it. Day after day, the Soviet-British-American propaganda machine has been telling the Indian people that Germany is out for world-domination and, in particular, for the domination of the Orient. I am alarmed to see how effective this propaganda is gradually proving to be.

Even prominent people who have spent their whole life in fighting England and have been in prison for long years, are being increasingly influenced by this propaganda and are thinking that if there is no hope of obtaining India's freedom through the help of the Axis, it is better to make peace with Britain on the best terms available. If this process is not arrested the time will soon come when the majority of the Indian people will definitely take their stand on the Soviet-Britain-American side. We cannot hope to bring India over to the side of the Axis, if the Axis Powers do not first declare their policy regarding India.

India is being prepared as the central military base of the British Empire. An army of one million men is being raised in India which will be fully equipped by modern war industries newly established there. If this plan succeeds, we have no doubt that even after the German occupation of England, the British Empire will carry on the war, using India as the base.

America is now playing an increasing role in the internal politics of Oriental countries e.g. of China, where she has brought about an agreement between Chiang-Kai-Shek and the Chinese Communist Party. With a new American Minister and an American Military Attache in India, America will also have a role in the internal politics of India. And if America succeeds in bringing about a similar compromise between Gandhi and the British Government, the position of the party standing for Independence and Revolution will be greatly weakened.

There is still time to save the situation in India, but if there is further delay in issuing the declaration regarding Indian Independence, I am afraid it will become extremely difficult for us to win over the Indian people to the side of the Axis. Once the majority of the Indian people go over definitely to the Soviet-British-American side, the declaration will no longer have any value for India.

Further, if there is no declaration regarding Indian Independence, the nearer the German armies move towards India, the more hostile will the Indian people become towards Germany. The march of the German troops towards the East will be regarded as the approach not of a friend, but of an enemy.

If, therefore, the declaration is to come at all, it should come *before* the German armies are moving further eastwards.

The new Anglo-Soviet guarantee to Turkey indicates that the British attack on Iran is imminent. The road to Afghanistan which has been open all these months will be out after the British occupy Iran and it will then be difficult for us to work out our plans regarding India. With Iran under British occupation, there will be one solid bloc under British control, stretching from the Mediterranean to Burma. The work in the Tribal Territory and in India will then be much more difficult than before.

The joint announcement made by President Roosevelt and Prime Minister Churchill regarding their programme of post-war reconstruction has been interpreted by the London radio to mean that India will get her freedom after the war. America has also decided to negotiate directly with the Dominions on outstanding problems of common interest, independently of Britain. All these facts further confirm the view that America will in future, intervene in the internal affairs of the British Empire and in consequence thereof a compromise between Gandhi and the British Government appears highly probable in the near future.

I fully realise the complexity of your problem and I certainly cannot expect your Excellency to do anything for India which may be considered prejudicial to your national interest. But India stands today at one of the crossroads of her history and the situation there is deteriorating day to day. If therefore we are to be effective in our work for India, we must act at once. I would, therefore, beg your Excellency not to leave us in suspense any longer but to come to an early decision, whatever that decision may be.

Thanking your Excellency,

Yours respectfully,

SUBHAS CHANDRA BOSE

11

Address Me as O. Mazzotta

Letter to Naomi Vetter, Autumn 1941

My dear Mrs. Vetter,

Through our common friends I have kept myself informed about you. Owing to the conditions under which I have been living here, it was not possible at first to get into touch with you. Afterwards, I heard of the terrible bereavement which overtook you. As there was a possibility of my going to Vienna, I decided not to write to you but to meet you personally when I was there. Unfortunately, when I arrived there, you were away. As I do not know if I shall be coming to Vienna in the near future, I am writing this letter. First of all, let me convey my sincerest condolences to you on your saddest bereavement. Since I had the privilege of knowing President Vetter so intimately and since I respected and admired him so much, I can appreciate the loss that you have suffered. In these hard times, may God give you strength to put up with all the trials that you are having to face.

There is much that I would like to talk to you about, if I could meet you. For that purpose a letter is not a suitable medium. Please let me know your present address, as well as your future movements so that I may look out for the possibility of meeting you personally. Before I conclude, I should like to thank you once again from the bottom of my heart for all the kindness I have received at your hands in the past.

Assuring you of my deepest esteem,

I am, yours ever sincerely,

Subhas Chandra Bose

P.S. Please address me on the cover as O. MAZZOTTA.

SCB

12

The Fall of Singapore

FIRST BROADCAST, 19 FEBRUARY 1941[1]

This is Subhas Chandra Bose speaking to you over the Azad Hind Radio.

For about a year I have waited in silence and patience for the march of events and now that the hour has struck, I come forward to speak. The fall of Singapore means the collapse of the British Empire, the end of the iniquitous regime which it has symbolised and the dawn of a new era in Indian history. The Indian people who have long suffered from the humiliation of a foreign yoke and have been ruined spiritually, culturally, politically and economically while under British domination must now offer their humble thanks to the Almighty for the auspicious event which bears for India the promise of life and freedom.

British Imperialism has in modern history been the most diabolical enemy of freedom and the most formidable obstacle to progress. Because of it, a very large section of mankind has been kept enslaved and in India alone, about one-fifth of the human race has been ruthlessly suppressed and persecuted. For other nations, British Imperialism may be the enemy of today, but for India, it is the eternal foe. Between these two there can be neither peace nor compromise. And the enemies of British Imperialism are today the natural allies of India—just as the allies of British Imperialism are today our natural enemies.

The outside world hears from time to time voices coming from India, claiming to speak either in the name of the Indian National Congress or of the Indian people. But these are voices coming through the channels of British propaganda and nobody should make the fatal

---

[1] This is the text of Netaji Subhas Chandra Bose's first broadcast to the world over the Azad Hind Radio on 19 February 1942. A slightly modified version of this broadcast was published as a statement in *Azad Hind* (No. 2, 1942).

mistake of regarding them as representative of Free India. As is natural in a land that has been under foreign domination, the British oppressors have endeavoured to create divisions among the Indian people. As a consequence thereof, we find in India those who openly support British Imperialism. There are others who, whether intentionally or unintentionally, help the British cause while often camouflaging their real motives by talking of cooperation with China, Russia and other Allies of England. There is, however, the vast majority of the Indian people who will have no compromise with British Imperialism but will fight on till full independence is achieved. Owing to war-time conditions prevailing in India, the voice of these freedom-loving Indians cannot cross the frontiers of that country— but we who have fought for more than two decades for our national emancipation, know exactly what the vast majority of our countrymen think and feel today.

Standing at one of the cross-roads of world-history, I solemnly declare on behalf of all freedom-loving Indians in India and abroad that we shall continue to fight British Imperialism till India is once again the mistress of her own destiny. During this struggle and in the reconstruction that will follow, we shall heartily cooperate with all those who will help us in overthrowing the common enemy. I am confident that in this sacred struggle, the vast majority of the Indian people will be with us. No manoeuvre, intrigue or conspiracy on the part of the agents of Anglo-American Imperialism, however prominent they may be and to whichever nationality they may belong, can throw dust in the eyes of the Indian people or swerve them from the path of patriotic duty. The hour of India's salvation is at hand. India will now rise and break the chains of servitude that have bound her so long. Through India's liberation will Asia and the world move forward towards the larger goal of human emancipation.

13

Seize This Opportunity

BROADCAST, 11 MARCH 1942[1]

Sisters and brothers!

For some time I have watched the changes in the world calmly and quietly. The fall of Singapore is a prelude to the fall of the British Empire. A new era is setting in. By enslaving us, the British have entirely ruined our morality and our finances. We bow our heads before God, who has granted us such an auspicious occasion for freeing India. In this age there is no greater enemy of freedom and progress than Britain. Now is the time to wake up from your slumber. The end of British domination will mean the end of a tyrannous regime, and the beginning of a new life in the history of India. The British have heaped indignities and humiliations upon us. Again we thank God for giving us this auspicious opportunity. Today many nations of the world are the enemies of Britain. The friends of Britain are our enemies.

The Indian National Congress claims to guide the nation. But its half-hearted measures have encouraged British leaders to continue to follow the old and hackneyed course, namely, of making promises without meaning to fulfil them. I also know that there are such people in India who are anxious to preserve the British Empire. The majority of Indians do not want either British rule or their economic system. We will not cease fighting until Mother India is free.

In the world is dawning a new age. A true patriot says that his own fate must be decided by himself. We are ready to co-operate with any nation that will help us in regaining our independence. I hope that all my Indian brothers and sisters will help me in this war against the British.

---

[1] Speech broadcast over Azad Hind Radio from north Germany on 11 March 1942.

Even with her cunning, and under-hand policy, Britain cannot fool India, neither can she stop Indians from cherishing their ideal of nationalism. India has decided to fight for her freedom. She will not only free herself, but will free Asia and even the whole world.

14

Burmese Freedom

BROACAST, 13 MARCH 1942[1]

Friends!

The fall of Singapore has been hastily followed by the collapse of other military bases of Britain's imperialistic Allies in East Asia. The Japanese capture of Rangoon has revived the hopes of freedom of the Burmese. They will again breathe a free atmosphere, just as they did when they were a free nation. The prophecy, which the German Foreign Minister made on 26 November 1941, is proving true. How prophetic were his words when he said that Britain would lose her military bases one by one. The British Empire stands threatened in every quarter. The flame of British glory is flickering. Their days are numbered.

As usual, the British have been, since the outbreak of the present hostilities, striving desperately to cajole other people into shedding their blood and supplying armaments to the British for the successful prosecution of the war. But their efforts have failed. They are facing disaster and disgrace on all fronts. The Indians have been, since September 1939, entreating the British Government to apply the principles of freedom and democracy to India, and thus give practical proof of their honesty and goodwill towards them. Some Indian nationalists even went to the extent of announcing that, should the British satisfy their national aspirations, they would be prepared to help them in this war. To this appeal British statesmen paid no heed. As a matter of fact, they never gave an unambiguous reply which would have earned the goodwill of Indians. With characteristic hypocrisy and fraud, they have again made an obscure declaration.

---

[1] Broadcast from Berlin on 13 March 1942.

Throughout their rule in India, the British have been seeking to create disunity among Indians. They have succeeded to some extent in this object, and on the plea of disunity among the various sections of the people, they have consistently refused to grant self-government to India. There is no end to British intrigues. Now they are uselessly making a lot of fuss over a possible enemy invasion of India. It has been frequently argued that India's frontiers lie on the Suez Canal and in Hong Kong. On this pretext, the British carried Indian troops to the Libyan desert and France and caused their bloodshed. In the East, the Indians were sacrificed in Hong Kong and Singapore in utter disregard of Indian wishes. Indian frontiers do not lie where Wavell has arbitrarily fixed them. This is only a mischievous invention of the British mind. India's geographical borders lie only where nature has created them. Britain, whether she is governed by Conservative or Labour leaders, like Churchill and Cripps, has been causing starvation in India. The Indians have been reduced to abject poverty. To ensure the safety of their Empire and to tighten the shackles of India's bondage, the British are demanding help and heavy sacrifices from her. They want the Indians to work like serfs and ceaselessly toil and fret for them.

The Indians understand that they have no enemy outside the Indian frontiers. The British have not changed their traditionally vicious policy. Indian troops are being recalled, since it is being said that the war is threatening the very gates of India. Here the question arises as to who is responsible for involving India in the war? Had not India's entry into the war been arbitrarily decided, her wealth and raw materials been tapped, her geographical situation been exploited for using her as a military base, and unlike Eire, her freedom of action been usurped, she would have never been a party to the present war. Every deceptive weapon was employed against her in order to convert her into a military base and to exact the greatest possible help from the Indians.
Friends!

The proper moment for valuing British manoeuvres at their real worth and for learning the nature of their tricks has arrived. They are only anxious to spread war to India which has already been made a belligerent country. No one should be surprised to learn of these age-old British tactics, in pursuance of which they have been continuously seeking to drag other nations into their war. Wherever the situation grew critical they deserted their Allies. In other words, they have been ruthlessly and systematically bringing ruin and disaster to mankind. Right from Dunkirk up to Batavia they have caused widespread destruction. Are not you Indians still convinced of British selfishness?

My Indian brothers, it is not worthwhile to hope that the British will ever be able to help you in keeping hostilities beyond the frontiers of India. Rather, they will continually undertake to destroy India, and will not desist from resorting to the 'scorched-earth' policy in your country as well. The British Empire was founded on relentless plundering of weak nations. So long as it is in their power they will persist in the exploitation of subject nations. If the Indians took it to their heart that their country should be safe from danger, their first duty would be to carry out a thorough destruction of British military objectives in India, and prevent India's raw material, wealth and youth from being harnessed by the British to their war effort.

Friends, it is crystal clear that in British decline alone lies the hope of India's independence. Every Indian who works to strengthen British hands, betrays the cause of his motherland. Such a man is a traitor to India. Whoever opposes Indian patriots and sides with the British is no better than a Mir Jafar or an Umi Chand of the present generation. Brothers and sisters,

Every one of you should understand that to come to terms with the British, who are about to perish, is a ridiculous commitment in the eyes of the world. Churchill has recently announced the possibility of granting Dominion Status to India as soon as it is feasible. He has commanded Cripps to go out to India in order to bring together the various Indian political parties, and to find out what measure of power should be granted to the Indians under the present circumstances. No sane Indian can be pleased with this latest British offer. Today, no Indian is prepared to trust empty British promises of freedom after the war. Every Indian politician knows that the British always aim at the policy of 'Divide and Rule' in India. So long as their foot remains on Indian soil they will never abandon their vicious policies. Churchill and his Government will, before long, come to realise that Indians can no longer be hoodwinked by them. Brothers and sisters, I am witnessing, with my own eyes, the downfall of the British Empire. If Cripps or any other British statesman comes out to India, the Indians cannot evince any interest in him.

In the present world struggle one group of nations is trying to maintain the power it achieved as a sequel to the Versailles Treaty. The other group of nations is fighting with an iron will to eradicate the unhappy state of affairs looming large in the world and to establish a 'New Order'. Brothers and sisters, you stand to lose only one thing from this war, and that is your shackles. Indians cannot be satisfied by the present rotten world order. They can be happy only in a new and a better scheme of things, which will rescue them from the jaws of destruction and serfdom. This war is bound to leave the British Empire in ruins and achieve that end.

The famous Tripartite pact has been concluded to put an end to tyrannical British imperialism. The parties to this pact are our comrades. It is absolutely ridiculous to say that a combination of Axis Powers constitutes a menace to the freedom of India. The facts are quite different. I know these nations fully well, and I can assure you that they have great sympathy for the cause of our freedom. If any one is doubtful on this point, he may be reminded of the recent statement of General Tojo, the Japanese Premier. Let me hope that my compatriots will no longer entertain any doubts about their goodwill towards us and yield to false Anglo-American propaganda. Indians should be delighted with the brilliant victories which the Japanese are scoring against their enemies. The day when justice and equality will assert themselves is not far off. When that time comes then alone will Indians be able to prosper and flourish in an atmosphere of freedom and justice.

Long live Revolution!

15

India has no Enemy Outside Her Own Frontiers

BROADCAST, 19 MARCH 1942[1]

Sisters and Brothers!

After the fall of the island-fortress of Singapore, the other bastions of British and Allied imperialism in the Far East have been rapidly surrendering. Rangoon has now fallen, and the Burmese people can once again breathe freely as they did in the days of old, when their land glittered with golden palaces and pagodas and their rich green fields smiled in prosperity. The words of Germany's Foreign Minister, uttered on 26 November 1941, have proved to be prophetic, and Britain is losing her positions one after another. Nothing is visible on the horizon that can possibly arrest the collapse and break-up of her vast Empire. Since the beginning of the present war, Britain, in accordance with her traditions, has sought to get other peoples and nations to fight her battles and also to provide the sinews of war. But these tactics have been unavailing, and Britain has, therefore, been beaten in every major conflict, whether in the west or in the east.

From September 1939 onwards, the Indian people have continuously appealed to the British Government to demonstrate their bonafides by applying the principles of freedom and democracy to India. Some nationalists have even gone so far as to offer their full support to Britain's war in the event of India's national demand being fulfilled. The only reply from the British side has been a refusal, not plain and blunt, as we would have preferred, but perfidious and hypocritical. The British, who have endeavoured to create dissensions among the Indian people

---

[1] Speech broadcast over Berlin Radio on 19 March 1942. It was also published as 'The Second Statement' in *Azad Hind* (No. 2, 1942).

throughout the period of their rule in India, have put forward these artificially engineered dissensions as an excuse for denying self-determination to India. Not content with such hypocrisy, British propagandists tried to persuade the Indian people that their country stood in danger of enemy attack, and that the frontiers of India were, therefore, at Suez and Hong Kong. On this pretext, Indian troops were forcibly sent right up to Libya and France on the West, and to Singapore and Hong Kong on the East, against the declared will of the Indian people. But as a matter of fact India has no imaginary Wavellian frontiers, she has a national geographical boundary determined by Providence and nature. It is only the British Empire that has frontiers extending from North to South and from East to West. And it is this Empire, whether ruled by a Conservative or by a Labour Cabinet, that has deprived the Indian people of life and liberty as well as bread and arms. To save such an Empire, and incidentally to ensure their own slavery, the Indian people have been asked to give their blood, toil, tears and sweat in unmeasured quantity, though in reality India has no enemy outside her own frontiers.

For some time past there has been a change in Britain's tactics. Indian and other troops are being sent to India and the people are being told that the war is now coming to India. But who has been moving earth and heaven to bring India into the war zone? If the British Government had not declared India a belligerent in September 1939, and had not tried by all means—fair and foul—to exploit the wealth, man-power, the raw materials and the industrial resources of India for feeding Britain's war machine—if the British Government had not converted India into a big military base—and if India had, on the contrary, been allowed to remain neutral, like Eire—there would have been no possibility of India coming within the arena of the present war. But by the most cunning procedure, Britain has endeavoured to drag India into the war-zone with a view to ultimately securing India's voluntary co-operation in Britain's selfish war efforts. It is, therefore, high time that the Indian people saw through the dirty game which British politicians are now playing, namely, to bring the *war into India*, just as in September 1939, they were responsible for bringing *India into the war*.

Such tactics, however, should not cause any surprise, because since 1939 the British have continually attempted to bring the war into other people's lands. From Norway to Crete and from Libya to Hong Kong, they have instigated and provoked other people to fight, and at the crucial hour they have themselves escaped, leaving others in the lurch as we have witnessed again and again from Dunkirk to Batavia. It is useless to expect the British to keep India out of the war-zone and out of the sufferings, misery and privation which modern war entails. In the course of military operations, they will not hesitate for one moment to apply the scorched-earth tactics to our own country. The Empire, which was born of robbery and greed and which thrives on injustice and oppression, will continue to exploit and terrorise so long as it survives. But if the Indian people want to keep their country out of the arena of war, they must themselves remove Britain's military base from India, and put an end to Britain's exploitation of India for imperialist war purposes.

The victory of the British Empire will mean the perpetuation of our own slavery, and only through the complete overthrow of that Empire is India's emancipation possible. Consequently, any Indian who now works for Britain acts against the best interests of his country and is a traitor to the cause of liberty. Indian nationalists will have to fight not only their imperialist rulers—but also the Lackeys of British Imperialism—the Mir Jaffars and Umi Chands of today. And to everybody, it should be clear as daylight that to think of compromise with an Empire that will soon disappear is not only futile but ridiculous.

The British Prime Minister, Mr Churchill, has in his recent utterance before Parliament promised Dominion Status to India as soon as possible after the war is over. Under his mandate, Sir Stafford Cripps is to visit India in order to bring about an agreement between the different sections of the people, and to decide what political concessions should be granted at present. Only one who lives in a fool's paradise could imagine that India still cares for Dominion Status within the Empire, and that a single Indian could be found who still has the least faith in British promises which are to be redeemed after the termination of the war. People in India know full well that the much advertised and so-called dissensions are an artificial creation, and that as long as the British remain in India they will continue their nefarious policy of 'divide and rule'. Mr Churchill and his Cabinet will soon realise that political promises thrown at the Indian people from Westminster will not bring them over to the British side. The British Empire is going the way of all other Empires of the past, and out of its ashes will rise a free and united India. The visit of Sir Stafford Cripps or of any other British politician at this late hour is, therefore, of no consequence to India, and will not arouse any interest in that country.

In the present Armageddon, there is a desperate attempt, on the one side, to maintain the status quo that has sprung out of the Treaty of Versailles, and similar treaties of the past—while on the other, there is the determination to destroy the old order and usher in a new one. In such a conflict, India has nothing to lose but her chains, and the hopes and aspirations of the Indian people can be fulfilled not through the maintenance, but only through the destruction of the old order, which signifies for them—humiliation, slavery and death.

Taking a bird's eye view of modern history, I feel convinced that as the last World War led to the dissolution of some old and decadent empires, so will this War culminate in the dismemberment of the British Empire, the last anachronism in modern politics. The Tripartite Powers—Germany, Italy and Japan—through whom this consummation will be brought about, are accordingly our natural friends and allies. It is the blackest lie to say that these Powers constitute a menace to India. From my intimate knowledge of these three nations, I can assert on the contrary that they have nothing but sympathy and goodwill for India and for Indian independence. If ever there was any doubt on this point, the recent historic declaration of the Prime Minister of Japan, General Tojo, should reassure my countrymen once for all, and no Indian should in future allow himself to be duped by British propaganda. Let us, therefore, rejoice that under the simultaneous blows of the Tripartite Powers, the British Empire, our eternal foe, is fast crumbling down. Let us rejoice over the rapid and victorious advance of the Japanese forces in the Far East. Let us rejoice that the old order which was set up at Versailles is crashing before our very eyes. And let us rejoice over the coming dawn which will bring for India—freedom and justice, happiness and prosperity.

Inquilab Zindabad! Azad Hind Zindabad!
(Long Live Revolution! Long Live Free India!)

16

My Death is Perhaps an Instance of Wishful Thinking

BROADCAST, 25 MARCH 1942[1]

This is Subhas Chandra Bose, who is still alive, speaking to you over the 'Azad Hind' radio. British news agencies have spread all over the world the report that I had died in an aeroplane crash on my way to Tokyo to attend an important conference there. Ever since I left India last year, British propaganda agencies have from time to time given contradictory reports of my whereabouts, while newspapers in England have not hesitated to use uncomplimentary language about myself. The latest report about my death is perhaps an instance of wishful thinking. I can imagine that the British Government would, at this critical hour in India's history, like to see me dead since they are now trying their level best to win India over to their side for the purpose of their imperialistic war.

I have not before me at the present moment the full particulars of the aeroplane disaster referred to above. I cannot, therefore, say if it was the result of sabotage on the part of our enemy. In any case, I beg to offer my respectful homage to the memory of those who lost their lives in that tragic event. Their names will be written in letters of gold in the history of our struggle for independence. They were the national heroes of India.

I have considered very carefully the offer of the British Government to India and the radio speech of Sir Stafford Cripps in that connection. I feel perfectly convinced that it is now quite clear that Sir Stafford has gone to India to try the age-long policy of British imperialism—'divide

---

[1] Broadcast over Azad Hind Radio (Germany) on 25 March 1942.

and rule'. Many people in India did not expect Sir Stafford Cripps to play a role which might very well have been reserved for a Conservative politician like Mr Amery. Sir Stafford has himself assured us that the terms offered to India are, in his opinion, the soundest and best, and that the members of the British Cabinet were all unanimous over these proposals.

This affords one further proof that, in Britain, all party differences disappear when the question of India comes up. Sir Stafford has told us that India is a sub-continent inhabited by many races and peoples. I would like to remind him that India was unified under the empire of Ashoka the Great, several centuries before the Christian era—more than 1,000 years before England was unified.

Britain has, in other parts of her Empire, for instance in Ireland and Palestine, used the religious issue in order to divide the people. She has been utilizing in India for that same purpose not only this issue but other imperial weapons like the Indian princes, Depressed Classes, etc. Now Sir Stafford is in India to use the same instrument for imperialistic ends. It is no less striking that Sir Stafford is applying the old imperialist policy of working for a compromise with one section of the people while simultaneously suppressing the other. That is why on the one side Sir Stafford is conferring with one set of politicians, while on the other the fearless and uncompromising fighters for independence are safely lodged behind prison bars. The Indian people are fully aware of this nefarious policy of British politicians. I have no doubt that the spirit of our freedom-fighters will hurl down the prison walls and inspire the people of India to know that this is an insult to India's self-respect and honour.

As the London paper, the *Daily Telegraph*, has remarked, Sir Stafford's proposals contain nothing that is fundamentally new. The essence is Dominion status within the Empire, which will be realised only when the war is over. But according to the terms of the offer, the speech of Sir Stafford Cripps and the comments of English papers like the *Manchester Guardian*, it is quite clear that the real intention of the British Government is to split India into a number of states, just as Ireland was split up at the end of the last war. I am doubtful whether India will even look at such an offer. Indians are by nature hospitable, and Sir Stafford will be committing a grievous mistake if he interpreted such hospitality to mean the acceptance of his offer.

Sir Stafford reached the height of imperialist hypocrisy when, at a press conference at Delhi, he remarked that Indians have not been able to produce an agreed constitution. But the Indian people know from their own bitter experience that only the British Government is responsible for the corruption and bribery in India. The Indian people are, therefore, convinced that they can no longer hope to win their freedom by discussion or argument, propaganda and passive resistance, but must now resort to other methods that are more effective and powerful.

Sir Stafford also mentioned that while the war is going on, a new constitution cannot be framed for India, and hence the inauguration of Dominion Status will begin on the termination of the war. I may remind Sir Stafford Cripps that, as early as October 1939, I replied to the British Government by suggesting that a Provisional National Government, commanding the confidence of the majority of the people, should be set up at once. This Provisional National Government could be made responsible to the present Indian Legislative Assembly. In other words, this Provisional National Government could be made responsible to the elected members of the Indian Assembly. This suggestion was first of all put forward by me on behalf of the Forward Bloc of the Congress, and it being practicable and reasonable, the official Congress Committee also adopted it as their own demand. The fact, however, is that the British Government is not ready to part with power at the present moment. By raising the issue of the minorities or of the Princes or of the so-called Depressed Classes they can at any time find a plea that Indians are not united. Sir Stafford must be living in a fool's paradise if he thinks that, by offering such hopeless offers, he can satisfy India's hunger for Freedom. In the last World War, with the help of India, the war was won by England, but India's reward was further suppression and massacre. India has not forgotten those episodes, and she will see also that the present golden opportunity is not lost.

Since the beginning of this century, the British Government has been using another organisation as a counterblast to the Congress in order to reject its demands. She has been using the Muslim League for this purpose, because that party is regarded as pro-British in its outlook. In fact, British propaganda has tried to create the impression that the Muslim League is almost as influential a body as Congress, and that it represents the majority of India's Muslims. This, however, is far from the truth. In reality there are several influential and important Muslim organisations which are thoroughly nationalist. Moreover out of the 11 provinces in British India out of which only 4 have a majority of Muslims, only one, the Punjab, has a Cabinet which may be regarded as a Muslim League Cabinet. But even the Punjab Premier is strongly opposed to the main programme of the Muslim League, namely the division of India. Consequently, it seems that the Muslim League only commands a majority in a single province of India. But even then it is said that the majority of the Muslims will not stand for Indian independence.

As far as the defence of India is concerned, it is stated in the British proposals that, so long as the war lasts, the full military control of India will be directly in the hands of Britain, not even in the hands of the Viceroy or the Commander-in-Chief in India. By this policy, Britain wants to achieve a two-fold purpose. She desires, on the one hand, to utilise to the fullest extent India's resources for the whole Empire, and, on the other, to force thereby the enemies of Britain to attack Britain's military base in India, so that the Indian people may be provoked into voluntarily entering the war as Britain's ally. I would like to affirm, with all the emphasis at my command, that all the pro-British Indians who are participating in Britain's war will alone be responsible if the war came ultimately to India. I would like further to warn my countrymen that Britain's sole object now is to drag the Indian people into the war. It has been a successful game of the British people to get other nations involved in the war. Up to the present time they have been carrying out glorious retreats and successful evacuations. Recently they have adopted a novel policy of burning and destroying everything before taking to their heels. If the British Government apply these scorched-earth tactics to their own country, that is no concern of ours. But I have every reason to believe that they have decided to apply these scorched-earth tactics in Ceylon and India, should the war come there. Therefore, participation in Britain's war will not only hinder Britain's defeat and overthrow, but will also delay the attainment of independence for Indians.

17

An Open Letter to Sir Stafford Cripps

BROADCAST, 31 MARCH 1942[1]

This is Subhas Chandra Bose speaking. I shall now address an open letter to Sir Stafford Cripps, in English.
Dear Sir Stafford Cripps,

The world has been told that you have undertaken a mission on behalf of the British Prime Minister and the Cabinet to go to India and try to save India for the British Empire. It is understandable that the present Prime Minister and the Cabinet should make use of you for this purpose. But it passes one's comprehension that you, Sir Stafford, should accept such a job. You are well aware of the reactionary character of the present Cabinet. The presence of Labourites in it does not alter its real character. Having been forced to keep company with the Labour Party some years ago, you perhaps know more than anybody how unprogressive that party is, particularly on questions dealing with India and other suppressed nations of the Empire. Mr Ramsay MacDonald's National Cabinet could at least claim to have Labour support, but even that is lacking in the present Cabinet.

In the days when you fought with the British Labour Party in vindication of your own principles and convictions, you commanded the admiration of many people including myself. You have been so anti-Imperialist in your outlook that you even advocated the abolition of the monarchy which has served as the corner-stone of British Imperialism. That fundamental position of yours has altered so radically that you accepted a portfolio under Mr Winston Churchill, than whom

---

[1] Broadcast over Azad Hind Radio (Germany) on 31 March 1942.

a more anti-Indian Englishman it is difficult to find in the whole of Britain. People who know you personally, or who have followed your career with interest, are consequently quite puzzled at your present political stand. One can easily understand Mr Churchill. He is an imperialist, believing in the policy of brute force and he makes no bones about it. Even the British Labour Party's attitude we can perhaps understand. British Labour leaders are in reality as imperialistic as the Conservatives are, though they may talk in a more polite and seductive manner. We have faced the Labour Party's administration in 1924 and again from 1929 to 1931.

On both these occasions we had to spend our time in British prisons, sometimes without any trial whatsoever. India will never forget that between 1929 and 1931 a Labour Cabinet was responsible for putting about 100,000 men and women into prison, for ordering large-scale lathi charges on men and women all over the country, for shooting down of defenceless crowds as in Peshawar, and for burning houses and dishonouring women as in the villages of Bengal. You were one of the sharpest critics of the Labour Party when in London in January 1938, I had the pleasure of making your acquaintance. But today you appear to be quite a different man.

You may perhaps say that your task is to bring about a reconciliation between India and England. But your Cabinet has made it perfectly clear that the offer to India is not one of independence but of Dominion Status within the Empire, and further, that Dominion Status will be promulgated not immediately but at the end of the war. You have just declared in Delhi that your attitude towards India is the same as that of Mr Churchill. We are grateful to you for such frankness, but are you not aware what the Indian people think of British promises? Are you not also aware that the history of British rule in India is a history of broken pledges and unredeemed promises? And knowing as you do that the Indian National Congress stands for undiluted independence is it not an insult to India that a man of your position and reputation should go out there with such an offer in his pocket? Another matter which has pained all patriotic Indians is that your programme is to get into touch with leaders of all possible parties in India, no matter whether they are representatives of the masses or individuals. You at least should be aware that some of these parties have so far been used by British politicians as a counter-blast to the Congress and in order to minimise its influence and importance. It is also surprising that you are reassuring the Princes that they have nothing to fear from the coming changes. Your work in respect of the Princes was already taken in hand by the Viceroy, Lord Linlithgow, in anticipation of your arrival. To a neutral observer, therefore, your role appears to be the same historic role of deceit and duplicity which British politicians have played in the past.

At the beginning of this war British politicians talked very loudly of freedom and democracy. At the same time, they have been bolstering up the claims of minorities in order to exaggerate India's differences, and thereby keep India under perpetual domination. The minorities problem is not something peculiar to India, it is to be found all the world over. If British politicians really believe in democracy why don't they apply the democratic solution to India and solve the Indian problem? British politicians and the British propaganda machine have been continually reminding us since 1939 that the Axis Powers are a menace to India and now we are being told that India is in danger of an attack by the enemy. But is not this sheer hypocrisy? India has no enemies outside her own frontiers. Her one enemy is British imperialism and the only adversary that India has to get rid of is the perpetual aggression of British imperialism. It was the British Government that declared India to be a belligerent power against the will of the Indian people and have since then been forcibly exploiting the resources of India for Britain's war purposes. Further, it was the same Government that interned and imprisoned in India the nationals of Germany, Italy and Japan after the outbreak of war. The Axis Powers and the Indian people realise that they are not at war with one another, and the former have not, therefore, imprisoned Indian nationals living in their countries, and have nothing but sympathy and goodwill for them. I am convinced that if India does not participate in Britain's war there is not the least possibility of India being attacked by any of the Axis Powers.

18

India for the Indians

BROADCAST, 6 APRIL 1942[1]

This is Subhas Chandra Bose speaking to you over the 'Azad Hind Radio' in reply to the historic declaration of the Prime Minister of Japan.

His Excellency the Prime Minister of Japan, General Tojo, has, after the fall of Singapore and of Rangoon, made two historic pronouncements on the Indian problem. These declarations are of such great significance that it is necessary for India to speak in reply what her attitude is. On behalf of all freedom loving Indians in India and abroad, I offer my sincere thanks to the Japanese Prime Minister for his outspoken sympathy for Indian independence. The slogan he has uttered, 'India for the Indians', will go down in history as the prophetic utterance of a far-seeing statesman. Ever since the Russo-Japanese war of 1904–5, the Indian people have looked upon the awakening in Japan with admiration. It was through Japan that Asia first asserted her self-respect and honour. A strong Japan, therefore, is in the best interests of Asia.

I welcome most heartily the statement of His Excellency the Prime Minister that Japan is determined to destroy completely the influence of Anglo-American imperialism in the East. Until this is done, Asia will be under a perpetual danger. Asia, and particularly India, will be forever grateful to the Tripartite Powers if they can dispose of this menace once for all. The present war which the Tripartite Powers are waging against Britain and America, is of vital interest to India, and the Indian people are, therefore, following with joy and satisfaction the continued defeats of the Anglo-American forces.

---

[1] Broadcast over Azad Hind Radio (Germany) on 6 April 1942 and printed in *Azad Hind* (3/4, 1942).

It will be wrong for me to ignore the fact that there is a certain section among the Indian people that is, for some reason or other, on the side of Britain. This is but natural in a country that has been so long under a foreign yoke. But I may say without the slightest exaggeration that the vast majority of the Indian people are burning with the desire to break their shackles of bondage. For them this war is a God-sent opportunity for realising their long-cherished dreams and aspirations.

The people of India remember quite clearly how they were deceived and betrayed by British politicians during the last World War. They have no desire to repeat that experience. They know that British rule in India has been one long record of broken pledges and unredeemed promises. They have, therefore, resolved to liquidate once for all the British regime in India, which was born of robbery and corruption and which has thrived on injustice and oppression. I can assure His Excellency the Prime Minister that India will not miss this golden opportunity, which is, indeed, rare in the lifetime of a nation.

The Indian people are today fully conscious that the two factors which were primarily responsible for her servitude were her isolation from the rest of the world and her internal disunity. This lesson, which they have learnt from bitter and painful experience, they will never forget. As in the old days, when India was a free, proud and progressive nation, so also in future will the Indian people live in the closest friendship with all the other nations of the world, and in particular with the Tripartite Powers, and thereby contribute to the common culture and civilisation of humanity. And it will be an honour and privilege for India to co-operate intimately with Japan in the noble task of creating a great Asia that will be free, happy and prosperous.

19

Compromise-Hunting is Like War-Mongering

BROADCAST, 13 APRIL 1942[1]

This is Subhas Chandra Bose speaking to you over the 'Azad Hind Radio' on the political situation in India. Sisters and brothers! It is rather painful to hear that even after the reactionary and monstrous character of the British proposals for India, it seems to the world that some of our countrymen are still carrying on laboured discussions with Mr Winston Churchill's envoy in India, Sir Stafford Cripps. Isolated from the military frontiers of India and poisoned by British propaganda, some of our people at home may not realise for the moment that the British Empire is now breaking up and that it will soon disappear from the face of the earth. Consequently, even if the British were to offer to India terms that are far more conciliatory than the present British proposals there is no meaning in entering into a compromise with such a power.

There is no Indian today who has the least faith in British promises, which are to be fulfilled at the end of the war. In the face of these difficulties, some of our liberal friends have endeavoured to facilitate a compromise by suggesting that the Governments of the Allied Powers and of the British Dominions should guarantee to India that Britain's promises will be redeemed when the war is over. But what value is there in such guarantees when we have no power to enforce their fulfillment? Have we forgotten what happened to President Wilson's Fourteen Points? Have we forgotten that President Roosevelt's envoy, Ronald Donovan, travelled all over the Balkans with letters from the President in his pocket urging the Balkan countries to declare war on the Axis

---

[1] Broadcast over Azad Hind Radio (Germany) on 13 April 1942 and printed in *Azad Hind* (3/4, 1942).

Powers? And have we forgotten that all these countries that were provoked and instigated into joining in the war were ultimately left to their fate by the all-promising President when the Axis forces overpowered them? I am sure that even if some people are still blind, the vast majority of our countrymen realise that the United States of America are playing a role of an agent provcateur and they regard themselves as the heirs of the British Empire that has gone into compulsory liquidation.

It is comical to see men who have been, and still are, slaves of the British suddenly developing megalomania in the company of men like Sir Stafford Cripps and Louis Johnson and then appointing themselves saviours of the British Empire. But no power on earth can save that Empire which is now going the way of all other Empires of the past. Even if India were to fight for Britain to the last man with all her resources, the overthrow of the latter cannot possibly be averted. Britain has to reap the unavoidable fruits of her past policy in keeping India enslaved and impoverished. And even if a National Government were to be set up in India tomorrow it could not possibly build up and equip a modern army during the course of the present war.

It is no less comical that the Indian saviours of British Imperialism are the men who regard themselves as international democrats. These estimable gentlemen shut their eyes to the fact that India's one and only enemy is British Imperialism. Simply because they are humoured and lionised by the wily British, they conveniently forget that India today lies under the heel of Britain and they talk of lining up with the progressive forces of the world. They do not talk frankly of cooperating with Britain but camouflage their real motives by asking the Indian people to co-operate with China or Russia or America. But such camouflage cannot deceive the Indian people who are fully aware that the British Empire does not represent a progressive force in this world and is in fact the citadel of reaction.

I consider it my duty to warn my countrymen that in the present crisis which faces India compromise-hunting is like war-mongering. The British have been using India as their military base partly because they want to provoke the Tripartite Powers into attacking India so that the Indian people may be ultimately persuaded to fight with Britain. The Tripartite Powers, on their part, have openly declared their sympathy for Indian Independence. They have no desire whatsoever of attacking neutral Ireland. Their only interest is to destroy Britain's military base in India without which the war cannot be brought to a victorious conclusion. To make a compromise with England now, on the basis of co-operation in Britain's war effort, is converting India into an enemy of the Tripartite Powers and forcing these powers to attack not only Britain's military base in India but all those Indians who co-operate in Britain's war effort. Let those who are now seeking a compromise with Britain realise that they are really working for bringing the war into India.

The immediate effect of a compromise will be more looting of India's wealth and resources by the greedy Englishman. It will be a declaration of war on the Tripartite Powers by the compromise hunters in India. And it will mean sharing England's imminent defeat and all the shame and humiliation that it will imply. And when the British flee the country on the eve of their defeat, just as General MacArthur and General Wavell have done elsewhere, they will burn and destroy everything in accordance with their new-fangled scorched-earth policy. When India is once brought into the war zone of our British and Indian war-mongers—not only will the people have to experience the horrors of war at home—but India's essential supplies of food and other materials which come from adjacent countries, will also be completely cut off.

Our countrymen will easily realise from a glance at the map how precarious Britain's position is today. Britain has been expelled from Europe. In Africa, after her preliminary victories, she is now on the retreat. The Near and Middle East, which has up till now been held under subjugation, is like a powder magazine and only a spark is needed to cause an explosion. In the Far East, she has been licked and kicked everywhere by the Japanese. Her only hope is, therefore, India, and that is why Sir Stafford Cripps is today at our door-step. But, India cannot save the Empire from its inevitable doom. She can either go down with that Empire or she can emancipate herself if she can spurn all offers and threats that may now come either from Whitehall or from the White House.

If Sir Stafford Cripps claims to be a friend of India, the best service he can now render is to keep India out of this war. India will then be able to look after herself and forge her own destiny.

The British have at long last realised that they do not enjoy any moral prestige in India. That is why they commandeered the services of Marshal Chiang Kai-shek and that is why Mr Louis Johnson has been rushed to India, carrying letters from the White House in his pocket. The Americans being the latest converts to Imperialism, employ not only the methods of conciliation, but also those of threat, warning the Indian people what dire disaster will overtake them if they do not respond to the advances made by Mr Winston Churchill's envoy.

I appeal to my countrymen not to be duped by British propaganda any longer. It will mean the biggest disaster for India if they walk into the trap laid for them by Allied politicians. India's destiny hangs in the balance. Our first duty is to prevent our land becoming the next theatre of war and we can do so only by refusing to co-operate with Britain in her imperialist war. I can assert with a full sense of responsibility that if India is not used as a military base for Britain, there is not the slightest possibility of any of the Tripartite Powers attacking India.

My next appeal to my countrymen is that after keeping the war out of India, they should without any delay renew the national struggle for independence and on a more intensified scale. Britain has turned down India's demand for immediate independence and it is now for India to fight for her own freedom. What better opportunity can one dream of for achieving India's emancipation?

In conclusion I want to tell my countrymen that we, who happen to be outside India, have not been idle all these months. We have been following the international situation with the closest interest and have also been preparing ourselves for the coming struggle—the final struggle—which will bring India to her cherished goal of liberty. We are aware that everywhere the British forces are on the run. We are aware that British sea-power, on which the Empire was built, has already become a legend of the past. We are aware that Britain has neither the air force nor the land force necessary for holding India in servitude. The day is therefore near when we shall have to march to India, in order to participate in the last struggle for our national liberation. The fight we shall then have to wage, will be not only with the armed forces of Britain—which at present are extremely weak in numbers—but also with all the allies of British Imperialism, whether Indian or foreign. And if British Imperialism can summon aid from all over the globe, in spite of its being a world power, there will be nothing wrong if we too ask for aid from quarters that are friendly to Indian Independence. Let our countrymen cease thinking of what is happening at New Delhi and let them, instead, prepare for the struggle ahead. To our comrades in prison, let them convey our message of good cheer. The day is not far when we shall be at their side. The Indian prison will then be stormed—the alien oppressors will be thrown out and India will once again be free.

20

My Allegiance

BROADCAST, 1 MAY 1942[1]

Sisters and Brothers!

I addressed you last on the occasion of the Jalianwalla Bagh Day, more than three weeks ago, and I then reminded you once again of the deceit and hypocrisy underlying the present policy of the British Government, which culminated in the journey of Sir Stafford Cripps to India. Sir Stafford offered, on the one hand, a promise of Dominion Status for the future, and on the other, he demanded the immediate co-operation in Britain's war effort. Strangely enough, the gallant knight expected the Indian people to accept such an absurd proposition. The contemptible British offer was, however, rejected unconditionally, and this was a matter of joy and pride to Indians in every part of the world.

I must, nevertheless, state that it was a painful surprise to find that after the departure of Sir Stafford Cripps from India and despite the refusal of the British Government to concede India's national demand, some prominent countrymen of ours have been publicly advocating a policy which amounts to unconditional co-operation with Britain in her war effort.

Is human memory so short that these gentlemen have forgotten the resolutions of the Indian National Congress from 1927 to 1938 which deal with the war? Did we not reaffirm year after year from 1927 to 1938 that when the next war comes we shall refuse to participate in it and that we shall resist every attempt on the part of the British Government to drag India into that war? In September 1939, when the present war broke out, did not the Indian National Congress deliberately

---

[1] Broadcast from Berlin on 1 May 1942 and printed in *Azad Hind* (3/4, 1942).

refuse to render unconditional co-operation to the British Government? And did not the Congress take disciplinary action against and expel from its ranks such a prominent leader as Mr M.N. Roy for the crime of advocating unconditional co-operation with the British Government? Mr M.N. Roy in those days said nothing more than what some followers of Mahatma Gandhi are now saying and we are therefore waiting to see what disciplinary action will be taken against these gentlemen who are so unceremoniously flouting the principle of the Congress. I also know that these new converts to the creed of co-operation will perhaps assert that they have altered their principle and policy in order to meet a new menace, the menace of aggression from without. But I would like to ask them if the aggression against which the Indian people have been fighting so long, the perpetual aggression of British Imperialism, has been successfully fought and destroyed. In spite of all that British propaganda has been saying or may say in future, it should be clear to all right thinking Indians that in this wide world India has but one enemy, the enemy that has robbed her of her freedom, the enemy that has exploited her for more than hundred years—the enemy that even today sits on the chest of Mother India and drinks her life-blood. That enemy is British Imperialism.

It is a moral tragedy that some of my countrymen have been so duped by British propaganda that they forget that real enemy, India's one and only enemy, that keeps India enslaved even now. These misguided people talk of aggression by Japan or Germany or Italy, without knowing at first hand what policy these powers have with regard to India.

Friends, I know something about these powers and their foreign policy. I have been in intimate and personal contact with them ever since I left my home more than a year ago and I can assure you with all seriousness and sincerity that these three Powers want to see India fully independent and as the mistress of her own destiny. These Powers, moreover, are determined to defeat and destroy British Imperialism. It is, therefore, the task of the rising generation of the Indian people, in whose hands rests the future of their country, to utilise the present international crisis to the fullest extent, so that out of the ashes of the British Empire may rise a free and united India. I am not an apologist of the Tripartite Powers and it is not my task to defend what they have done or may do in future. That is a task which devolves on these nations themselves and they are quite able to deal with it. My concern, however, is with India; and it is my duty as a patriotic Indian to inform my countrymen as to how best we can achieve the liberation of India in the present world crisis, without meddling in the internal affairs of other countries.

In the present international crisis the logic of history has made the enemies of British Imperialism our closest friends and allies. If British Imperialism is defeated and annihilated, India will win her freedom. If, on the other hand, British Imperialism were somehow to win the war which, however, is quite impossible, then India's slavery will be perpetuated forever. India is, therefore, presented with the choice between freedom and slavery and she must take her choice in favour of freedom. For the Indians of today, it is the chance of a lifetime and for India it is an opportunity rare in human history.

Friends, I have laughed whenever I have heard Britain's paid propagandists calling me an enemy agent. *I need no credentials when I speak to my own people.* My whole life, which has been one long, consistent and continuous record of uncompromising struggle against British Imperialism, is the best guarantee of my bona fides. Perhaps better than any other living Indian of today, I know foreigners and foreign politics and I have known Britishers from my very childhood. If the Britishers who are the past masters in the art of diplomacy and political seduction, have in spite of their best efforts, failed to tempt, corrupt or mislead me, no other power on earth can do so. All my life I have been a servant of India and till the last hours of my life I shall remain one. *My allegiance and my loyalty has ever been and will* ever be to India and to India alone, no matter in which part of the world *I may live at any given time.*

British propagandists, who have been well nigh silenced by Prime Minister Tojo's historical declaration of 'India for the Indians' have now fallen back on their last argument, which is drawn from the Sino-Japanese struggle. They are now shouting from the house-tops 'see what the Japanese have done in China.' I may tell these propagandists, both British and Indian, that when I was the President of the Indian National Congress I was responsible for giving effect to the Congress resolution to send a goodwill mission to China. Those were the days when Marshal Chiang Kai-shek was fighting for his nationalist principles and that was why he could win the sympathy of Indians in an overwhelming degree. But the Marshal, who came to India the other day to ask the Indian people to fight for England, was quite a different man, a puppet of the Anglo-American Powers. And, the Japan that the Marshal is now fighting is quite a different Japan, a Japan that is at war with Britain and America, a Japan that is determined to annihilate Anglo-American Imperialism in the East, a Japan with whom Marshal Chiang Kai-shek can come to an honourable understanding today, if only he can emancipate himself from the grips of his Anglo-American masters.

Friends, think for a moment, therefore, where India stands today. Do you want to dig your political grave by still hanging on to a power that will soon cease to exist? Is it not better, far better and wiser, to accept the hand of friendship, that has been offered you by the Tripartite powers and that found remarkable expression in the historic and epoch-making declarations of the Prime Minister of Japan? Some of our arm-chair politicians may shout: 'We shall not take the help of any foreign power!' Friends, nobody compels you to take the help of foreign power for achieving your political emancipation. Do not take that help, if you do not need it; but if you do need it, there is no harm if you take it. I have studied very closely modern history during the last 200 years, and I have studied in particular the history of all the fights for freedom during this period, but I have not as yet found one single instance, where freedom has been won, without foreign aid or alliance in some form or other. And do you not see with your own eyes, what Britain has been doing herself? This Almighty British Empire, over which the sun did not set, has been going round the world, with the begging-bowl, asking for men, money and munitions, not only from the free nations of the world, but also from enslaved countries like India. If there is nothing wrong in Britain begging for help, there can be nothing wrong in India accepting an offer of assistance, if she needs it. And if the Britishers can welcome Americans, coming to India to assist them, we too should heartily welcome any friends who may come to India, to help us in the last struggle against British Imperialism.

Friends, since I spoke to you last, you have noticed how the British Government, under the plea of fighting Japanese aggression, has opened the door to American aggression. American diplomats, American businessmen and American Army units are now overrunning India, and if this process is not arrested at once, we shall soon have a new peril to face. The British Empire has been sent into compulsory liquidation by the Masters of White House and Wall Street, and the latter are now doing everything possible to gradually take over the British Empire, even while the war is going on.

The Viceroy of India has in his broadcast of 7th May appealed to you to set up a national war-front. Friends, His Excellency has given you wholesome advice. Sink all your differenceas and put up a common front against India's eternal foe. His Excellency was also right when he told you that you must rouse the will to unite and the will to act. For the coming struggle, we must also strengthen the public morale and ruthlessly eliminate all those who seek to undermine it, by talking of compromise and co-operation. His Excellency has, no doubt, refused to give you the necessary arms. But that does not matter. The arms will reach your hands in the nick of time. Meanwhile get everything ready for there is not a minute to lose—and send a word of good cheer to all our comrades in prison. We are thinking of them day and night. Tell them that they will be the first to taste the joy of freedom, when the expected hour arrives.

Friends and countrymen, when the British Empire is disappearing amidst the sands of time and the fate of India hangs in the balance, I want to remind you that in this month of May and on the 10th day of that month in the year 1857, began India's first war of independence. In May 1942, 85 years later, has begun India's last war of independence. Friends, gird up your loins, the Hour of India's salvation is at hand. We Indians, who are outside India, have been preparing for this, the last phase of our national struggle. We have been preparing not only for the armed struggle that will soon take place, for the liberation of our dear motherland, but we have been preparing, also, to face and to solve the problems of post-war reconstruction in Free India. The Azad Hind Sangh as an international organisation will be soon at your side to fight and win India's liberty and then build up a Free India. I assure you that Free India will have full freedom to determine her own form of Government, without any interference from any foreign power. Free India will have a social order based on the eternal principles of justice, equality and brotherhood. And, last but not least, Free India, AZAD HIND, will be a land of free, happy and prosperous men and women, who will take their place in the comity of free nations.

21

I Should be in the East

LETTER TO GERMAN FOREIGN MINISTER
VON RIBBENTROP, 22 MAY 1942

> Berlin-Charlottenburg 2
> Sophienstr. 6–7
> 22 May 1942

Your Excellency,

Your Excellency is aware of the rapid developments in the Far East which have brought the Japanese forces to the frontiers of India. These developments have had their repercussions on events inside India, where conditions are now ripe for a revolution. India has now the opportunity to overthrow the British yoke and win her liberty—an opportunity which is rare in history. I, therefore, feel that I must make the fullest use of this unique opportunity.

Looking back upon my stay here for little more than a year, I think that I have done some useful and enduring work for my country. But now the time has come when the final effort should be made for achieving India's political emancipation. For this purpose, it is absolutely essential that I should be in the East. Only when I am there, shall I be able to direct the revolution along the right channels.

I am profoundly grateful to the German Government—and to Your Excellency in particular—for the hospitality, assistance and kind consideration that I have received during my stay in Germany. This has served to forge the ties that will bind us together for all time. I am convinced more than ever before that the Tripartite Powers and India have a common destiny. Our common goal—the final defeat of Anglo-American Imperialism—demands that I should now go to the East and from close quarters guide the Indian revolution towards that goal. Not only the cause of India, but our common cause as well, will be best served by my presence in the East, at a place, as near to India as possible.

During my absence from Europe, the organisation which your Excellency has helped me to set up here, will continue to work in the closest collaboration with the German Government. And I shall, of course, remain in intimate contact with my organisation here, as also with the German Government, through German Legations and German friends in the East.

It is now technically possible to travel to the East and both the German and Italian Governments are in a position to afford me the necessary facilities in this connection.

I am sure that Your Excellency, as well as the Führer, will appreciate this imperative and objective requirement of the revolutionary situation in India. I, therefore, confidently trust that Your Excellency will be good enough to provide me with the facilities necessary for traveling to the East, so that I may perform my duty towards my country, as a leader of the national revolution.

Assuring Your Excellency of my warmest esteem and with profound thanks,

I am,

Yours respectfully,
SUBHAS CHANDRA BOSE

22

Face to Face with the German Führer

RECORD OF THE CONFERENCE
BETWEEN HITLER AND BOSE, 29 MAY 1942[1]

Berlin, 30 May 1942

Record of the Conference between the Führer and the Indian Nationalist leader

Bose on 29 May 1942[2]

Present: Federal Foreign Minister, Secretary of State Keppler, Ambassador Hewel

At the outset Bose greeted the Führer as an old revolutionary and thanked him for the honour bestowed upon him by this reception. The day would forever remain as a historical date in his life. He thanked the

---

[1] This is a free English translation of the official account of Netaji's interview with Hitler from the archives of the Foreign Office of the Federal Republic of Germany, obtained in microfilm for the library of Netaji Research Bureau and later published in 'Staatsmaenner und Diplomaten bei Hitler', Part two, Ed. Andreas Hillgrueber, Bernard & Graefe fuer Weh rwesen, Frankfurt am Main, 1970.—Eds.

[2] In the original record of Hitler's official interpreter Paul Schmidt, filed with the office of the Foreign Minister, the date of the meeting is given as 27 May 1942. From other sources, viz. records of the supreme Command of the Wehrmacht, 'The Fuehrer's Diary', and the report of German News Bureau (DNB), it is clear that the conference took place on 29 May 1942. As to the place of the meeting, the original record mentions the Führer's headquarters, which is also not correct. The meeting took place in the Reich Chancellory in Berlin.—Eds.

Führer for the hospitality and the kindness shown to him by the German Government ever since his arrival more than a year ago, as also for the help received by him in his work for the liberation of his country and in the formation of an Indian Legion. When he had left India the previous year in January, his colleagues had been very worried about his personal fate and about the possibilities of serving the Indian cause. He (Bose) had however been driven to this course by instinct and deliberation. Looking back, he felt certain today that he had acted in the best interests of his country. The help of the 'Tripartite Powers' was necessary for India, even though the actual war of independence had to be fought out by India herself. While India must do her duty in this war, she also needed the sympathetic support of the external world.

The time had now come for taking up the question of military collaboration with the Japanese armed forces. India attached a lot of importance to establishing the closest relationship with Germany and Italy and be assured of the sympathy and help of these countries, because she did not want to be left to the resources of Japan alone.

Bose then came to the topic of his journey to East Asia. This, he said, was motivated by the desire to find a point as close to India as possible, from where the Indian revolution could be directed. Of course, during his absence from Germany, propaganda would be carried on by his trusted men he would leave behind.

Finally Bose came up with the request that the Führer should give him (Bose) some advice as an old and experienced revolutionary. Even though India was situated very far from Germany and the situation there was very different from that in Europe, there must be certain basic principles on the basis of which all revolutions had to be carried out.

The image of India had always been distorted and presented in an unfavorable light by British propaganda. The India, which he (Bose) represented, was not the old philosophical one, but a new modern and active India.

In this reply the Führer gave a brief description of the situation. Germany and India had the same merciless opponents. In the first place, there was England, which was ruling India and which had also ruled Europe by influencing inner-European discord and wanted to continue her rule. It was clear that this danger could be eliminated only by the military defeat of England, which would decisively deprive her of the power of exercising such an influence any further. Besides the British, the Bolsheviks and the Americans were also common enemies. Moreover, England, America and Russia were not playing a clean game with one another. America wanted to take over the legacy of England, and Russia again hoped to be the successor of both. For Germany and India it was immaterial whether America took over the legacy of England or whether the Russians in the final analysis deceived both the Anglo-Saxon countries. In India one should not shut one's eyes to the Russian danger, and certain friendly views of Pandit Nehru regarding the Russians appeared extremely dangerous to him (the Führer).

The distance between Germany and India was enormous. Though the opponents of both countries were the same, the war against them was being waged on battlefields, which were very far from one another. In spite of this distance India would clearly feel the effect of Germany's victory in Europe. Without the successes of Germany during the last two and half years, it could hardly have been possible for Japan to make such progress in East Asia, let alone the question of entering the war. India and Germany were therefore fighting the same battle against the same enemies, absolutely irrespective of where they met them.

India now had the one and only opportunity to shake off the English yoke without falling into the hands of the Russians, because Russia would now be completely smashed by Germany.

The battle in which Germany was involved was conducted by him (Führer) not as a propaganda war as a politician, but essentially as a means of power politics as a soldier. In this connection he (the Führer) allowed himself to be guided by the principle of not making any false prophecies. He had never promised anything, which was beyond the range of his own effectiveness. In internal affairs as well, he had always avoided predicting victory when it lay beyond the range of possibilities of his own power.

For these reasons he refrained from making any prophecies about Egypt at the present time. Since the day before that day Rommel had gone into the attack. He could not visualise whether this operation would lead to the disintegration of the British front. In any case, Germany would do everything, which lay within her power. She could not give anything more than its blood and labour. Should Rommel achieve only limited success, a comprehensive statement now about the fate of Egypt would only cause damage. If, however, Rommel succeeded in defeating the opponent, then one would be able to draw necessary conclusions. He (the Führer) would then at once appeal to the Egyptians to throw off the British yoke. In that case he could make such an appeal to the Egyptian people with a clear conscience; because the German power resources would back up such an appeal.

He (the Führer) had always been very careful about proclamations regarding violent overthrow of foreign powers. With regard to his own home Austria, he had therefore issued a proclamation to the Austrians only on the 12th of March 1938, i.e. one day before the marching in. A politician, who wanted to be taken seriously, could not act otherwise.

He was taking the same attitude in regard to the Arabian question. If Germany had already reached the south Caucasus and if she had half a dozen armoured divisions and a few motorised divisions at its disposal for sending help to the Egyptian and Arabian revolutionaries, he would not have hesitated to issue a proclamation to the Arabs. But now, with Germany still one thousand kilometres away from Arabia, such a proclamation would be irresponsible. He (the Führer) was no Englishman. He did not want to ruin other nations through proclamations. He was not working for the defeat of Egypt and the revolutionary Arabs, but wanted to help them to real success. He did not want to have a diversionary operation carried out by them, as Englishmen would do. Germany would give its own blood for its own cause.

The time for considering an appeal to Egypt under these circumstances could come in three months or only in one to two years, in any case only after Germany would have concentrated enough battle-strength at the gates of Egypt, to ensure the liberation of the country. The same held good for Arabia.

India was endlessly far from Germany. The only possibilities of communication with India was by land or air. Land communication would be via the Persian Gulf if the southern route was chosen; in the north, however, it would be via Afghanistan. In any case, the path would be only over the corpse of Russia.

He considered Japan's astonishingly rapid advance to be the historical event of the world of the last half-year, by means of which, her armies had practically advanced to the borders of India. Japan's aim was not known to him (the Führer). He did not know whether the Japanese considered it more important first to relieve their flanks from being threatened by Chiang-Kai-Shek or to seek a rapprochement with him, or whether they first wanted to turn to Australia or India. The defeat of their power in East Asia would possibly lead to the collapse of the British Empire. Such a collapse would naturally mean a great relief for Germany and would spare her a lot of blood. Thereafter, Germany would follow the sequence of events in East Asia with keen interest and it was her wish to help as far as possible from her side. This she would do by hitting the British wherever she found them. In this connection the Führer referred to the submarine battles, which would prove to be of indirect help also for the war in East Asia, just like the air attacks on British industrial centres and the war in North Africa. Each defeated English division there would liberate Indian forces, and the Indian forces which were held captive in them could later be put into action for the war of liberation of the Indians.

Germany could not do anything more at the moment. If, however, Germany could gain access to the borders of India like Japan, which would probably take another one to two years, then he (the Führer) would have requested Bose to stay with him, march into India with the German troops and subsequently kindle the revolution against the British.

However, under the circumstances prevailing at the moment he (the Führer) could only advise Bose to bank on the Japanese to project the revolutionary war from the Indian borders into the country itself. As an old revolutionary he could only give Bose the advice to quickly exploit the chance of an internal revolution in India with the enemy pressure from outside. He believed that neither the anti-fascist and anti-national socialist trends of thought of Nehru nor the passive resistance of Gandhi would pay off in the long run. British power could be smashed only if the Indian nation rebelled simultaneously with an external attack. Such an upheaval could be best organised from as close a position to the country concerned as possible. Hence it would be best for Bose to take up his position at such a point, which would be nearest to India and from where the strongest military pressure could be exerted on the Britishers. He (the Führer) did not know whether the Japanese actually wanted to exert this pressure. They had not mentioned anything positive to Germany.

In other respects he did not believe that a revolt alone, without external help, could bring the Indians freedom. As an old revolutionary he knew that with the progress in the field of modern arms even a relatively small number of troops, properly organised and backed by the decision to make full use of their weapons, could keep a big country in check. Only with the help of external military pressure would it be possible for the internal revolutionary forces to hinder reinforcements and transportation of troops by disrupting communication lines and thus contribute to the military collapse.

As matters stood, it would take at least another one to two years before Germany could gain a direct influence in India. Japan's influence, on the other hand, would come about in a few months. Therefore, Bose should negotiate with the Japanese, not only for influencing events in his motherland, but also for restraining the Japanese themselves from committing psychological mistakes by appropriate advice.

However the Führer warned Bose against an air journey, which could compel him to a forced landing in British territory. He (Bose) was too important a personality to let his life be endangered by such an experiment. One had to chalk out a safer path for him. A Japanese submarine had at that time arrived in Europe and could take Bose along in case it was returning soon. Otherwise, he (the Führer) would place a German submarine at his disposal, which would take him to Bangkok. With the help of a map the Führer then explained to Bose the probable route of the journey round the Cape of Good Hope and put the duration of the journey at approximately six weeks. In this connection he also explained to Bose how the communication routes from England and America to India and Russia could be cut off by the laying of submarine barricades between Natal and West Africa as also in the vicinity of Madagascar and India.

During the further course of the conservation Bose brought up two more requests. The statements made by the Führer in 'Mein Kampf' and on other occasions had been greatly distorted by British propaganda and were being used for propaganda against Germany. Hence he requested the Führer to say something clarifying Germany's attitude towards India at a suitable opportunity. This would clear up things as far as the Indian nation was concerned. Bose further requested afresh for the moral and diplomatic support of Germany for India, so that she need not have to depend on Japan alone.

In his reply to this question the Führer defined India's task as follows: Elimination of British influence, avoidance of Russian influence, efforts to come to some sort of agreement with Japan about India's eastern border, and finally internal organisation and reconstruction of India with the purpose of achieving Indian unity. This would be a time-consuming task, which according to the analogy of restoration of German unity would probably take one hundred to two hundred years.

Regarding Bose's comment about distorted reproduction of his own statements the Führer explained that he had previously taken a stand solely against certain tendencies according to which the subject nations were supposed to build up a united front against the oppressors. In view of the weakness of these nations he considered this to be completely wrong, especially also because the same circles which stood for such a policy in Germany also recommended a sort of passive resistance for the Reich of the Indian pattern, which in any case was a completely wrong doctrine.

About the question of Germany's support for India after the war the Führer remarked that it would hereafter consist of only economic support. Bose should not forget that the power of a country could only be exercised within the range of its sword.

At the time of parting the Führer extended his best wishes to Bose for the success of his journey and plans.

SCHMIDT

23

Statement to the World Press

June 1942[1]

Gentlemen!

I have great pleasure in meeting you, the representatives of the world press, and I greet you with all my heart, as one who has been a journalist himself and knows something about the importance of the press in public affairs.

I shall attempt to facilitate our contact by making a short statement answering some of the questions that you would perhaps like to put to me.

My journey from India has no doubt been an adventurous one, but it has not been very difficult, because our friends today are many and the channels of communication with India are several. It is no longer possible for Britain and her Secret Service to guard the long frontiers of India and when the right moment comes, nobody will be able to prevent my getting into India again.

My plan of escape from India was not the product of one single brain. The whole scheme was discussed at great length and after being decided upon, it was carefully planned in great detail. I am here today in accordance with the wishes of a very large section of the Indian people and whatever work I have done since leaving home, has found their fullest support. I am in constant touch, not only with public opinion in India but also with those individuals and circles whose assistance and support I need for our national liberation. I regard myself as servant of the Indian nation and my present task is to lead the fight for India's independence. But as soon as India is free, it will be the duty of the Indian people to decide what form of Government they desire and who should guide the future Indian state. I certainly have my own ideas

---

[1] Printed in *Azad Hind* (5/6, 1942).

regarding post-war reconstruction in Free India, but it will be for Free India to decide upon them. So long as I remain outside my country, I shall not do anything which will not meet with the widest approval of nationalist circles in India.

You will easily understand that I cannot at this stage say more about my journey—but I may tell you that before reaching Berlin, I have travelled a lot and have seen a good bit of the world. Regarding my whereabouts in future, I can only state that the plans of a revolutionary must always be adapted to the circumstances of the moment and to the needs of the situation in which he is interested.

I was greatly amused at the news of my death a few month ago. It was a clumsy piece of British propaganda which defeated its own purpose and I am sure that British propagandists do not feel happy about it now.

Since leaving India, there have been two principal objectives before me: firstly, to find out what is really happening in this world, quite apart from partisan propaganda; and secondly, to find out if India has any friends and allies abroad.

My own objective study and my personal observation of events in Asia, America and Europe have led me to the irresistible conclusion that Britain will lose the war and that the break-up of the British Empire is not only inevitable but is near at hand.

Regarding the second point, I was familiar in India with British propaganda conducted against Tripartite Powers and I was therefore particularly anxious to find out the truth for myself. My own experience has now convinced me that by the logic of history the Tripartite Powers have become our natural friends and allies. Every blow struck at the British Empire is a help to India in her fight for freedom while every effort to save the British Empire is an attempt to perpetuate India's slavery.

My conversation with Herr Hitler and Signor Mussolini will naturally remain confidential, but I may state quite frankly that they as well as the head of the Japanese Government are the best friends that the Indian people have, outside India, in their fight against British Imperialism.

Regarding the internal situation in India I would request you not to be carried away by British propaganda, Among the Indian people, the vast majority is hostile to the British Government and is eager to break the chains of bondage. There is, however, a small minority that is supporting the British Government in its war-efforts. Among the Indian nationalists, though there are sometimes differences in speed and also in method, all are united on the question of Independence. I do not regard any Indian nationalist as a political opponent, though I regard myself as the vanguard of the national army.

With the failure of Sir Stafford Cripps in India, Britain has lost her last chance of coming to an understanding with the Indian people. Now it is clear to them that freedom will not come, so long as the British Empire is not dismembered. Consequently, all Indian nationalists must now work for the overthrow of the British Empire. In this struggle, some nationalists may fight only with the weapon of civil disobedience or passive resistance, but those who stand with me, will not hesitate to draw the sword when the time comes. The British Empire has organised a strong combination of powers, with a view to maintaining the status quo and keeping India enslaved. Foreign troops and foreign war-materials are being poured into India from the British Empire, America, Africa and China. In such circumstances, it is the right and the duty of the Indian people to accept help that is offered them, no matter from which source it may come.

With the departure of Sir Stafford Cripps from India began the last phase of India's national struggle. Since then, the unrest has been gathering in volume and intensity and it will, before long, reach the boiling point. I have no illusions about the difficult task that awaits us in India. Nevertheless, British power is so weak today that I am perfectly confident that, given the right leadership and the necessary assistance, it is possible for the Indian people to overthrow the British yoke and liberate themselves once for all. The coming months will prove the correctness of this statement.

I know that British propagandists have called me names because I have challenged their lying statement that the Tripartite Powers are the enemy of India and because I have asserted that India's only enemy is British Imperialism. But I do not mind, since abuse is only a sign of weakness.

I am convinced that during the course of this war, India will be free. The freedom of India will mean the expulsion of Anglo-American Imperialism from Asia and it will afford a powerful stimulus to freedom movements all over the world.

24

The Pledge of the INA

ADDRESS TO THE INDIAN LEGION IN EUROPE AND BROADCAST, JUNE 1942[1]

Brave soldiers! Today you have taken an oath that you will give fight to the enemy till the last breath of your life, under the national tricolour. From today you are the soldiers of the Indian National Army of Free India. You have volunteered to shoulder the responsibility of forty crores of Indians. From today your mind, might and money belong to the Indian Nation.

Friends, you have the honour to be the pioneer soldiers of Azad Hind Fauj. Your names will be written in golden letters in the history of Free India. Every soldier who is martyred in this holy war will have a monument in Free India. The coming generations will shower flowers on those monuments. You are very fortunate that you have got this valuable opportunity to serve your motherland. Although we are performing this ceremony in a foreign land, our heads and hearts are in our country. You should remember that your military and political responsibilities are increasing day by day and you must be ready to shoulder them competently. The drum of Indian Independence has been sounded. We have to prepare for the battle ahead. We should prepare ourselves as early as possible so that we can perform the duties we have shouldered. I assure you that the time is not far off when you will have to put to use the military skill which you possess.

Today we are taking the vow of independence under the National Flag. A time will come when you will salute this flag in the Red Fort.

---

[1] Address to the Indian Legion in Europe, and broadcast on Azad Hind Radio, June 1942.

But remember that you will have to pay the price of freedom. Freedom can never be had by begging. It has to be got by force. Its price is blood. We will not beg freedom from any foreign country. We shall achieve freedom by paying its price. It does not matter how much price we have to pay for it. I assure you that I shall lead the army when we march to India together. The news of the ceremony that we are performing here has reached India. It will encourage the patriots at home, who are fighting empty-handed against the British. Throughout my life it was my ambition to equip an army that will capture freedom from the enemy. Today I congratulate you because the honour of such an army belongs to you. With this I close my speech. May God be with you and give you strength to fulfil the pledge which you have taken voluntarily today. Inquilab Zindabad! (Long Live Revolution!)

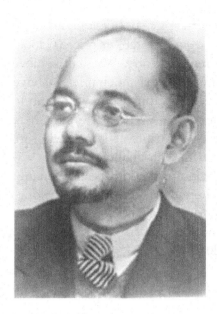

Figure 1 Subhas Bose on his arrival in Berlin, April 1941.

different individuals and
organisations claim to be
Leftists, how are we to decide
who are — and who are not —
genuine Leftists?
In the present political
phase of Indian life,
Leftism means Anti-Imperialism. A genuine anti-
imperialist is one who
believes in undiluted Independence
(not Mahatma Gandhi's substance of
Independence) as the political
objective and in uncompromising
national struggle as the means
for attaining it. After the attainment of political independence,
Leftism will mean Socialism and
the task before the people will
then be the reconstruction of
national life on a socialist
basis. Socialism or socialist

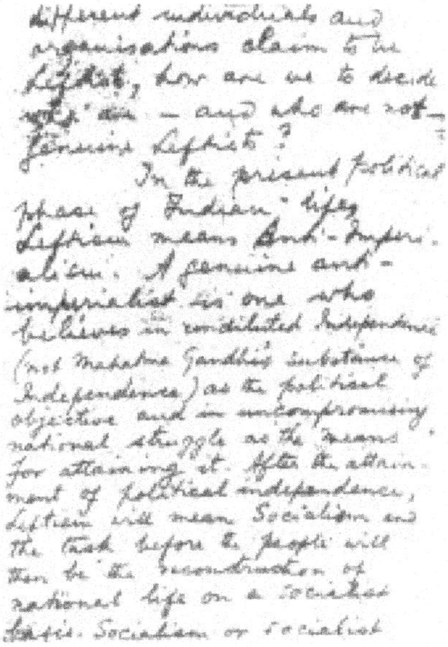

Figure 2 A page from the Kabul Thesis.

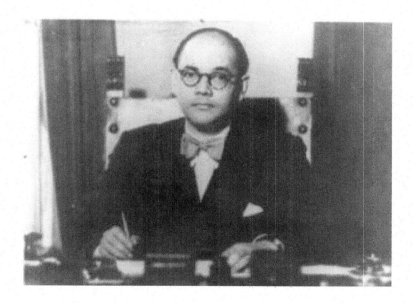

Figure 3 Subhas Bose at his desk, working under the cover name 'Orlando Mazzotta'.

Figure 4 Subhas Bose with the First Officers' Corps of Indian Legion in Europe.

Figure 5 A portrait, Berlin, 1942.

Figure 6 Subhas Bose at his desk in Berlin, 1942.

Figure 7 Subhas Bose speaking at the inauguration of the Indo-German Friendship Society in Hamburg, 1942.

Figure 8 In the garden of his house in Berlin.

Figure 9 Subhas Bose addressing the Indian Independence Day meeting in Berlin, 26 January 1943.

Figure 10 Subhas Bose with Abid Hasan on the submarine.

25

Link up Indian Nationalists All Over the World

MESSAGE TO THE BANGKOK CONFERENCE,
15 JUNE 1942[1]

I am delighted to have your message inviting me to your Conference which is going to meet under the distinguished Presidentship of the revolutionary leader Rash Behari Bose. Since it is not possible to join you in person, I must content myself with sending you this message conveying my most cordial greetings. The branches of the Azad Hind Sangh in Europe also associate with me in sending this message.

After Stafford Cripps' departure from India, the last phase in our national struggle has begun. In this historic struggle all nationalists, whether in India or outside, must play their part. The experience I have gained during the last 18 months has convinced me that in our fight against British Imperialism the Tripartite Powers are our best friends and allies outside India and I have no doubt that they will gladly render us such assistance as we may need. But the emancipation of India must be the work primarily of Indians themselves. We who are the vanguard of the National Army have the sacred mission of leading the national struggle to a successful conclusion. Though I have clear and definite views regarding post-war reconstruction in India, it is the Indian people in Free India who must determine the future destiny of the country and of the Free State.

My own objective study and observation in different parts of the world for 18 months has led me to the irresistible conclusion that Britain

---

[1] Message to the President of the Reception Committee of the Bangkok Conference, 15 June 1942.

will lose this war and that the British Empire will be completely dismembered. All the forces that are striving to destroy or weaken the British Empire are helping Indian emancipation while all forces that are endeavouring to save the British Empire are the forces that are attempting to perpetuate India's slavery.

It is a matter of profound gratification to all nationalists outside India that all nationalists inside India are united in the aim of India's Independence. We, who form the vanguard of the national army feel however that the time will soon come when it will be necessary to take up arms in the final stage of the struggle, And we also feel that since the British Empire is seeking help all over the world and is trying to flood India with foreign soldiers and foreign war material, it is the right and duty of the Indian nationalists to accept help that may be offered to them. Given the right leadership and the necessary capacity, the Indian people will undoubtedly be able to overcome all obstacles and will gain their freedom. When the crucial moment arrives nobody will be able to prevent my entering India again with a view to participating in the final struggle.

I am convinced that during the course of this war India will be free. India's liberation will mean the expulsion of Anglo-American Imperialism, the goal of the victorious Japanese Army. The freedom of India will also afford powerful stimulus to freedom movements all over the world.

I am glad to find that the branches of the Azad Hind Sangh in Europe are doing their very best to participate in the national struggle and are preparing for the post-war reconstruction that will follow. It is now time to link up Indian nationalists all over the world in one all-embracing organisation. I wish all success to your conference and I ardently hope and trust that it will prove to be a further mile-stone in our march towards victory.

Inquilab Zindabad
Azad Hind Zindabad!'
(Long Live Revolution!
Long Live Free India!)

SUBHAS CHANDRA BOSE

26

Differentiate between Internal and External Policy

BROADCAST, 17 JUNE 1942[1]

Countrymen and friends!

About five weeks ago, I addressed you last over the Radio—the Azad Hind Radio. Since then, I have travelled quite a lot and I am now in the very heart of Germany. Through the courtesy of the Berlin Short Wave Station, I therefore desire to address you again on the present international crisis.

First of all, I must congratulate you most warmly on your sense of national honour and self-respect in rejecting the impudent offer of Sir Stafford Cripps. By doing so, you have not only brought India nearer to the goal of liberty, but you have, at the same time, raised yourselves in the estimation of the whole world. As a consequence, India today stands in the front-line of world politics.

After the departure of Sir Stafford Cripps from India, an attempt was made by some of our prominent men to secure India's participation in Britain's war, even without a prior settlement with Britain over India's national demand. If this attempt had succeeded, the Indian people would have been shamelessly betrayed. But thanks to the pressure of public opinion and the opposition of Mahatma Gandhi, that danger has been averted once for all. It is now crystal clear that the Indian people will not participate in Britain's war. The only problem that remains to be solved is as to what positive steps they should take in order to achieve their liberation.

---

[1] Broadcast over Berlin Short Wave Station on 17 June 1942, and printed in *Azad Hind* (5/6, 1942).

The first move in this connection has already been made by the Indian public and by Mahatma Gandhi, by demanding that the Anglo-American forces should withdraw from India, so that there may be no possibility of India becoming a battle-ground in future. We have now to follow this up by preparing concrete plans as to what we should do, if the British Government does not respond to this demand.

It is a matter of profound gratification that Indian public opinion has registered its emphatic protest against the application of the scorched-earth policy to India. Once again, Mahatma Gandhi has risen to the occasion, by firmly voicing his protest in this important affair. But mere protest and agitation will not do. The Indian people must devise concrete measures for preventing the wanton destruction of their property when the British Army is forced to withdraw from India.

Friends! When I took the unusual step of defying the British Government and embarking from India, my principal objectives were two-fold—firstly, to find out for myself the truth as to what is happening in the world, and secondly, to see if India has any allies in her fight for freedom. During the time that I have been away from home, I have seen with my own eyes and heard with my own ears and I have followed closely the propaganda conducted by both sides in this world-war. I am, therefore, able to form an impartial and objective opinion as to what is happening now and what is going to happen in future. After this long, laborious and critical study of world-affairs, there is not the slightest possibility of being misled or misguided in my judgment. I should also like to add that whatever I have done since leaving home, or whatever I may do in future, has been—and will be—done with the sole purpose of bringing about the speedy emancipation of my country. And I shall never, do anything which will not meet with the approval of nationalist circles in India. Further I may say that if the cunning and unscrupulous and resourceful British Government has failed to allure or to corrupt me—no power on earth will ever be able to do so. Wherever I may happen to be, my one and only loyalty will be to India and to India alone.

Since coming to Europe, I have also seen much with my own eyes and I can therefore compare the actual conditions with the lies that are propagated from day to day by the B.B.C.—the Bluff and Bluster Corporation of London. Believe me when I say that Britain is going to lose the war—and as a sequel to her crushing defeat, the British Empire will be completely dismembered. Whether we actively assist Britain or whether we remain strictly neutral, nothing can alter by a hair's breadth the ultimate issue of this titanic struggle. In such a situation, it is not only wise and prudent, but imperatively necessary, for India to play a dynamic role. India must, by her efforts and by her sacrifice, contribute materially to the break-up of the British Empire, so that out of the ashes of that Empire may emerge a free and triumphant India which will be the creation of the Indian people.

It would be an act of political suicide to remain inactive or neutral in this crisis. If we do so, we shall either remain enslaved in spite of the dismemberment of the British Empire, or we shall receive freedom as a gift from the victorious Tripartite Powers. We want neither. The Indian people must therefore fight for and win their liberty.

But in this fight, some help from abroad is necessary. I have studied very carefully the struggle for liberty that has gone on all over the world during the last two hundred years—but I have not as yet discovered one single instance where freedom was won without outside help of some sort. Where the enemy is a powerful world-empire, the need for help is even greater. And where that powerful world-empire—namely Britain—is buttressed by a combination of several other powers, it would be the height of folly not to accept any assistance that may be offered us. When Britain has been pouring into India war-time materials and soldiers from America, China, Africa and the rest of the British Empire, it does not lie in the mouth of a Britisher to complain if we take help from any other quarter. It will, of course, be for India to decide what help she needs—and the less she needs it, the better it will be for her.

We can expect help or assistance only from those who are our friends and allies. In the present case, those who are trying to overthrow the British Empire are working for our liberation and are our friends and allies—while all those who are trying to save that empire are only attempting to perpetuate our slavery. But apart from this theoretical proposition, personal experience as well as the interviews with Herr Hitler and Signor Mussolini have convinced me that in the struggle against British Imperialism, the Tripartite Powers are our best friends and allies, outside India.

I know that friends like Swami Sahajanand may hesitate to believe in the sincerity of the Tripartite Powers. But I would like to remind them that these Powers have, in their own interest, resolved to fight British Imperialism to a finish and they will undoubtedly do so. Moreover, the whole world, including the Tripartite Powers, would stand to gain if India could liberate herself—and the only country to regret India's emancipation would be Britain.

In this fateful hour in India's history, it would be a grievous mistake to be carried away by ideological considerations alone. The internal politics of Germany or Italy or Japan do not concern us—they are the concern of the people of those countries. But even a child should understand that whatever the internal politics of the Tripartite Powers may be, their role in the international sphere is the destruction of the British Empire—which is India's one and only enemy. Do we not see with our own eyes how, regardless of ideological considerations, the British Empire is now co-operating with Soviet Russia?

It is high time that my friends and colleagues at home learnt to differentiate between the internal and external policy of Free India. The internal policy of Free India is, and should be, the concern of the Indian people themselves—while the external policy should be one of collaboration with the enemies of Britain. While standing for full collaboration with the Tripartite Powers in the external sphere—I stand for absolute self-determination for India where her national affairs are concerned and I shall never tolerate any interference in the internal policy of the Free Indian State. So far as socio-economic problems are concerned, my views are exactly what they were when I was at home—and no one should make the mistake of concluding that external collaboration with the Tripartite Powers means acceptance of their domination or even of their ideology in our internal affairs.

My task today is to lead the final struggle for India's emancipation. But when that task is fulfilled and India is liberated, it will then be my duty to report to my countrymen and leave it to them to decide what form of Government they would like to have. And as I told Mahatma Gandhi in my farewell talk with him in June 1940, before I was taken to prison—I shall again call on him when I have succeeded in my mission to achieve India's liberation from the British yoke.

Friends! it is a matter of joy and pride for all of us that, backed by the full diplomatic support of the Tripartite Powers, our countrymen in the Far East are now assembling in a Conference at Bangkok in order to devise ways and means for effecting the speedy emancipation of our motherland. As I have so often said, the last phase of our national struggle began with the departure of Sir Stafford Cripps from India. We shall soon reach a stage when we shall have to take up arms, if the Anglo-American forces do not voluntarily vacate India. Prepare for that auspicious day and organise simultaneously an anti-scorched-earth League all over the country for resisting wanton destruction by Bruisers before they fly from India.

Friends! The British Empire today is in such a tottering condition that I feel convinced that with the right leadership and the necessary assistance, it is possible for the Indian people to achieve their own salvation. This salvation will not be long in coming. In the course of the present war, India will win her freedom. And I repeat once again that when the hour strikes, I shall be at your side, ready to participate in the final struggle. The power that could not prevent my getting out of India will not be able to prevent my getting in. Meanwhile, please send a word of cheer to our comrades in prison. Let them patiently bide their time—for when the dawn of liberty comes, they will be the first to hail it. And we shall then bring them the arms and the equipment which will enable them also to be soldiers in India's last war of Independence.

Inquilab Zindabad!
(Long Live Revolution!)
Azad Hind Zindabad!
(Long Live Free Hindustan)

27

Full Support to Gandhi

EARLY AUGUST 1942[1]

The offer of the British Government which Sir Stafford Cripps brought to India was, in essence, a promise of Dominion Status after the termination of the war, with the possibility that India would be divided into two or more states, in accordance with the Pakistan plan of the Muslim League. This offer was rejected by the Indian people.

Sir Stafford Cripps left India on the 14th April after the failure of his mission. On his return to England, he obtained the support of all the British political parties and of the American press and public. To a section of the Indian public not yet completely disillusioned about Britain and America, it appeared surprisingly strange that Labour in Britain and the Democrat-Liberals in America did not support the Indian demands, but went out of their way to condemm the Indian people for rejecting the absurd offer of Cripps.

To hide his failure, Sir Stafford Cripps began to boast in England that he had at least succeeded in rallying all sections of the Indian public in active support of an anti-Axis policy. This claim of his was, at first, corroborated by a new stand suddenly taken by Pandit Jawaharlal Nehru. Nehru's declaration was to the effect that though no compromise had been effected between Britain and India, it was nevertheless India's duty and interest to actively assist in the fight against the Tripartite Powers. His policy amounted, in practice, to unconditional support to the Allied war-effort. Nehru, however, failed to carry any section of the

---

[1] Printed in *Azad Hind* (5/6, 1942). This article was written before the meeting of the All India Congress Committee on 7 August, and the arrest of Mahatma Gandhi and other leaders on 9 August.

Indian National Congress with him and when the All India Congress Committee (a body of about 400 representatives) met at Allahabad, towards the end of April last, it followed the lead of Mahatma Gandhi, as against that of Nehru. The main points in the resolution passed by the All India Congress Committee were as follows:

1. The Congress cannot consider any proposals which do not concede the full independence of India.
2. India cannot win her freedom through the intervention of, or invasion by, any other foreign power.
3. If any foreign power invades India, it should be resisted, but only by non-violent methods.
4. The Congress disapproves of the British policy of bringing foreign troops to India.

In view of this resolution, Sir Stafford Cripps could no longer maintain his claim that he had won over the Indian public to an active support of an anti-Axis policy.

For a time, Nehru stood as a lone figure, with nobody in the nationalist ranks to support his policy. Then he began to move towards Gandhi once again.

Anglo-American propaganda throughout the world continued to be active during the following months—supporting the policy of the British Government and condemning the Congress for its supposed intransigence. Even spokesmen and agents of Chungking began to speak in a similar strain.

The pro-British elements among the Indian people rigorously continued their work in support of Britain's war-effort. In order to strengthen their hands and weaken the resistance to the British Government, further strong measures were taken against uncompromising nationalists. As a matter of fact when a large number of Congressmen, headed by President Azad and Pandit Nehru, who followed Gandhi's lead, were released from prison in December 1941, other Congressmen who would not think of any compromise with Britain were left to rot in jail. During Sir Stafford's stay in India, while he was daily conferring with some Congressmen who had been recently liberated, other Congressmen who were uncompromising, were being taken to prison day after day. And when Cripps left India, these arrests continued. The brunt of this persecution fell on the shoulders of the Forward Bloc—the Left Wing of the Congress. This was in accordance with the well-known British policy—'Rally the Moderates but suppress the Extremists.'

Among the leaders of the Forward Bloc who are in prison—the majority without any trial whatsoever—are Sardar Sardul Singh Cavesheer, Acting President; Sarat Chandra Bose, Leader of the Congress Party in Bengal; Ruikar, Ex-President of the All India Trade Union Congress; Kamat, formerly of the Indian Civil Service; Bapat of Maharashtra; V. D. Tripathi of U. P.; Main Akbar Shah of the Frontier Province; Abdur Rahman of Kerala (Calicut); Annapurnaiah of Andhra (Madras Presidency) etc.

The above policy of the British Government reached its climax when the Forward Bloc was declared an illegal body (on the 23rd of June 1942).

Since May 1942, Gandhi had been finding himself in a difficult position. The pro-British elements knew their mind and they had been going their way. The uncompromising nationalists, too, knew their mind and they had been going on with their plan of fighting Britain by all possible means, without any thought of a comprise. Between these extremes, Gandhi was marking time. But a policy of marking time if continued long, means death for any political party. Consequently, Gandhi had ultimately to end the stalemate, if he did not want to stultify himself completely. And when he saw that there were no signs of a fresh move from the British side, he took a definite stand. At his instance, the Working Committee (Executive Committee of fifteen members) of the Congress passed a resolution at Wardha on the 14th July 1942, declaring—among other things—that British rule should be withdrawn from India.

After the departure of Cripps from India, Nehru became, for a time, the favorite of the Anglo-Americans, since he was advocating active support to the Allied Powers. But since then, he has been incurring their displeasure and wrath. He began by condemning the scorched-earth policy of the British Government and then took up the slogan that the British should clear out of India, as their presence would otherwise serve as a 'casus belli' to the Tripartite Powers. At the moment of writing, the British have concentrated all their anger on him, because he has not only issued the threat of civil disobedience (or Satyagraha or passive resistance), but has also made full preparations for translating that threat into action, if British rule is not withdrawn from India.

The resolution of the Working Committee which will come up before the All India Congress Committee at Bombay, on the 7th August 1942, should be situated carefully because it gives a clue to the mind of its author. The following paragraphs in that resolution are noteworthy:

'The freedom of India is thus necessary, not only in the interest of India but also for the safety of the world and for ending militarism, and other forms of imperialism, and the aggression of one nation over another . . .

Congress is anxious to avoid the experience of Malaya, Singapore, and Burma, and desires to build up resistance to any aggression or invasion of India by the Japanese or any foreign Power.

Congress would change the present ill-will against Britain to goodwill and make India a willing partner in the joint enterprise of securing freedom for the nations and the peoples of the world and in the trials and tribulations which accompany it. This is only possible if India feels the glow of freedom . . .

In making the proposal of the withdrawal of British rule from India, Congress has no desire whatever to embarrass Great Britain or the Allied Powers in their prosecution of the war, or in any way to encourage aggression on India or, of course, pressure on China by the Japanese, or any other power associated with the Axis group. Nor is it the Congress intention to jeopardise the defensive capacity of the Allied Powers.

Congress is therefore agreeable to the stationing of the armed forces of the allies in India should they so desire in order to ward off and resist Japanese or other aggression and to protect and help China.

The proposal for the withdrawal of British power from India was never intended to mean the physical withdrawal of all Britons from India, and certainly not those who would make India their home and live there as citizens and as equals with others. If such a withdrawal takes place with goodwill, it would result in establishing a stable provisional Government in India, and cooperation between this Government and the United Nations in resisting aggression and helping China.'

One should not suffer from any fond illusion that the Congress resolution shuts the door on a compromise and means war to the bitter end. On the contrary, prominent followers of the Mahatma have made transparently clear statements after the resolution was passed on the 14th July, pointing out that the Congress was offering cooperation in the Allied war-effort and was appealing to the United Nations to intervene in the Indian question. The statements of the Congress President, Abul Kalam Azad (who, by the way, is a Mohammedan) and of Sardar Vallabhbhai Patel are particularly important. It should not be forgotten that though Patel is hardly known outside India, within the Gandhi-Wing of the Congress he is the Mahatma's right hand.

At this stage I must remind the reader that when one refers to the Congress, one means the majority-group within the Congress—viz. the Gandhi-Wing. Though the majority alone can speak in the name of the Congress, there is, nevertheless, the other wing—the Left Wing of the Forward Bloc—which may today be a minority within the Congress, but which is really responsible for bringing the Gandhi-Wing round to an openly anti-British policy.

That no compromise between the Congress and the British Government has taken place is not because the former is opposed to it, but because the latter is not prepared to grant the minimum that is needed for making a compromise possible. On an intelligent analysis, it will be seen that what the Congress resolution demands is, in reality, independence on paper. Under that agreement the Allied Powers could station armies in India and operate against the Tripartite Powers from military bases within India. The Allied Powers could also demand the cooperation of the new Indian Government in the war which would mean, in practice, that the British Government—or the Allied Powers—could, with the consent of the Congress, prolong their occupation of India and ultimately drag India into the war as a willing partner.

From the point of the British, they would have everything to gain by such a compromise as envisaged by the above resolution. But Britain has fallen on evil days and statesmanship or farsightedness is no longer a quality possessed by British politicians.

Britain is still ruled by the Conservative Party and, in spite of pressure from Washington and Chungking, British Conservatives do not want to compromise with the Congress. Their reasons are as follows:

1. They are fighting to maintain their Empire. Without India the Empire has no meaning. Consequently, if India is to be given her independence, there is no point in carrying on the war.
2. They still hope to win the war and once they win the war, they hope to crush the Indian movement for liberty.
3. The British plan for solving the Indian problem after the war is Pakistan—that is, dividing India into several states.
4. The Conservatives think that in the middle of the war, a compromise with Gandhi will not bring them any appreciable advantages for increasing the war-effort. They think that they are already getting what help they can out of India. Further, the average Britisher is instinctively opposed to the idea of 'changing horses in mid-stream' and does not like big constitutional changes while the war is going on.
5. A recognition of Indian Independence, even on paper, will create endless complications for the British Government in future—especially, when they have other plans up their sleeves, for a post-war solution of the Indian problem.

In anticipation of the meeting of the All India Congress Committee on the 7th August 1942, the Anglo-American propaganda machinery has been in full swing since the middle of July. Every pro-British individual or group in India has been forced to come out in open condemnation of the above resolution. Outside India, every effort is being made to rally support for the British Government in case ruthless measures have to be adopted for suppressing the civil disobedience campaign. Over and above this, the Anglo-American Press has, from day to day, been threatening the Indian people with dire consequences if they make trouble. But all propaganda inside India by nondescripts cannot affect the position of the Congress in the least—while blackmailing propaganda from outside serves only to stiffen Indian public opinion against the British.

There is no doubt that the All India Congress Committee will ratify the Working Committee's resolution with a big majority. There is no doubt, either, that the Congress will secure tremendous support from the masses. But from my experience of the big campaigns of 1921 and 1930–2, I must say that there is always the danger of the situation being mishandled by Gandhi at a later stage. The late Deshbandhu C.R. Das who knew the Mahatma very intimately and who had eclipsed him from 1923 till his death in 1925, once told the writer that Gandhi always began a campaign brilliantly, but often ended in muddle. Apart from this, there is the consideration not to be easily set aside, that non-violent civil disobedience cannot secure the expulsion of the British from India. Therefore, while giving our full support to Gandhi in his demand for the immediate withdrawal of British rule, we should be careful in our attitude towards the whole campaign. The line which the Forward Bloc has adopted towards the Congress resolution and the campaign of civil disobedience is as follows:

1. Giving strong support to Gandhi in his demand for the withdrawal of the British from India and condemn all those who attack Gandhi.
2. Tell the Indian people that they should not think of a compromise with Britain at any stage—even if Britain were to offer one and some of the Indian leaders were to agree to it.
3. Tell the Indian people that stationing the Allied Armies in India is tantamount to declaring war on the Tripartite Powers and provoking them to attack Allied military bases in India. Consequently, demand for withdrawal of British rule should include the physical withdrawal of Allied Armies from India and also of all British officials. Without such physical withdrawal, the Independence we shall get will be Independence on paper.
4. Tell the Indian people that if passive resistance fails to secure the liberation of the country, they should be ready to take up arms in the final struggle.
5. Warn the Indian people that appeal to the United Nations is useless. The United Nations mean in reality Britain and America—the other nations being mere puppets. In the last war, the whole world was deceived by Wilson's Fourteen Points, though Wilson was personally an idealist. The Atlantic Charter of the Imperialist Roosevelt will betray humanity even more.
6. Tell the Indian people that India can, under no circumstances, offer cooperation in the war, as the price of independence. India can, at most, offer to be neutral, if Britain recognises her independence. This should satisfy Britain and, more than this, India should not offer—otherwise the war will be dragged into India by the Indians themselves.

There is not the slightest doubt that the British today are very nervous over the crisis in India, coming as it does at a time when the situation in Egypt is well-nigh precarious for them. They know, of course, that they, if they are sufficiently bloody and brutal, can crush, for a time, the campaign in India. Nevertheless, they are extremely worried for the following reasons:

1. To use bloody methods in India at such a time, makes it difficult for them to pose as the champions of freedom and democracy in the world.
2. A campaign in India which in peace-time would have been a flea-bite, becomes a serious affair in the present critical condition of the British Empire.
3. Civil commotion and unrest in India may affect war-production and also influence the moral of the Indian Army.
4. Civil Disobedience Campaign may so embitter the Indian people that they may like to ask for help from foreign powers and such help it is possible to secure now.
5. Even if the civil disobedience campaign be put down by force, it would not be easy for Britain to face an attack on British power in India from a first-class modern army when the Indian people are themselves in a strongly anti-British mood.

On the eve of the meeting of the All India Congress Committee due at Bombay on the 7th August, the British Broadcasting Corporation and its sister-stations all over the world, have started a terrific propaganda against Gandhi. According to these agencies, Gandhi's crime is that in the original resolution of the Congress Working Committee which met on the 27th April last, he had said that Free India could negotiate with Japan. This resolution of Gandhi's was amended at the instance of Nehru.

I have read the original resolution of Gandhi very carefully. There is nothing altogether new in it—because Gandhi has, from time to time, written in his journal 'Harijan', on somewhat the same lines as in the above resolution. The B.B.C. is, however, making a big fuss over this resolution for four reasons. It wants to tell the Allied Powers and their people that it is impossible to accept the Congress demand for British withdrawal from India by insinuating that Gandhi desires to make peace with Japan and give her concessions in India. Simultaneously, the British Government wants to make out a moral argument for denying freedom to India while professing to fight for freedom and democracy in the world. Thirdly, the British want to justify themselves before the bar of world opinion for adopting stern and bloody measures in India. And lastly, the British authorities want to give the political opponents of Gandhi a handle in their propaganda against his campaign of Civil Disobedience.

The cunning endeavour on the part of the B.B.C. to paint Gandhi as something like a secret Axis agent will fail miserably. Inside India it will not cut any ice at all while outside India, nobody who knows anything about Gandhi will attach the slightest importance to it. Congress circles in India already knew about Gandhi's resolution and for them it was no disclosure at all.

For the outside world, this so-called disclosure of the B.B.C. will give the impression that Gandhi is not an ideological fanatic like Nehru and is more of a realist than the latter. Nehru is fanatically anti-Axis and—left to himself—he would go to any length in order to fight the Tripartite Powers. His fundamental principle today is his anti-Axis ideology. With Gandhi on the other hand, the starting point is his non-violence. Because non-violent civil-disobedience cannot bring independence, Gandhi has to think of a compromise with Britain. And because he wants a compromise, he must refrain from a pro-Axis policy. A pro-Axis policy will naturally mean a final and complete break with England.

Gandhi not being an ideological fanatic, it is possible to influence him. There is not the slightest doubt that he has been influenced by the objective military situation and also by the propaganda of the Forward Bloc. The line he has indicated in the above resolution of his is, on many points, in accord with the policy advocated by the Forward Bloc since September 1939. Today, I am reminded of the last long talk I had with him in June 1940, at his village home near Wardha, just before I was taken to prison. From the position he then took up to the position indicated in the above resolution—is indeed a long way. And let us not forget that on the 6th September 1939, Gandhi had declared publicly that India should cooperate with Britain in the war!

But however much we may feel happy over the change that has overtaken Gandhi and over the success of our own propaganda, let us not expect the impossible. It is too much to expect Gandhi to openly advocate a pro-Axis policy. He is caught in the wheels of his own non-violent machine, which prevents his adopting such a policy.

The Civil Disobedience campaign will start in due course. We must give it our full support. But before this campaign begins to slacken down, it must be given a new turn. And through new and more effective methods, the independence movement must be carried on, till the British are thrown out of India and full emancipation is achieved.

28

The Quit India Movement

BROADCAST, 17 AUGUST 1942[1]

Friends!

The British authorities are always loath to admit that there is political unrest in India. In reporting popular disturbance, they always minimise the gravity of the situation and attempt to conceal facts that are prejudicial to their prestige. Nevertheless, Anglo-American agencies have been forced to give out that there has been trouble in several places in India—e.g. in Bombay, Ahmedabad, Delhi, Poona, Lucknow, Allahabad, Madras, Patna, Madurai, Agra, Moradabad, Nagpur, Cawnpore, Karachi, Calcutta, Secunderabad, Wardha, Dacca, Tenali, Jaipur, Amraoti, Ramnad, Masulipatam and Rawalpindi. Bombay has so far been the storm-centre of this great upheaval. The British authorities have also admitted that in Bombay alone, the police had to open fire on unarmed crowds ten times during the course of one day. But even that was not enough and in the evening, the police had to resort to shooting again. The casualties in Bombay for one day were 27 killed and 189 injured. The casualties in Delhi were 40 killed and 55 wounded. From such British admission, one can easily form a correct picture of what is happening in India today.

Reports coming in from independent and neutral sources indicate that India is now in a state of rebellion. There are meetings and processions everywhere in defiance of the official ban. In Delhi and other places crowds have marched towards Government House with the object of demanding that the Britishers should quit the land. In

---

[1] Broadcast on Azad Hind Radio on 17 August 1942 and printed in *Azad Hind*, 7/8 (1942).

many centres, the factory-workers have gone on strike and then the authorities have tried to coerce the workers. Large-scale picketing at railway stations and working-class quarters has taken place, which has led to an open clash with the armed police. Shops and business houses were closed all over the country as a protest against the arrest of the leaders. Students of schools and colleges have come out into the streets in enthusiastic support of the national demand for independence. Newspapers published by Englishmen which have condemned the Congress and its campaigns of civil disobedience have been burnt in thousands—and to replace them, bulletins published secretly by Congressmen have been distributed among the police. Postal stamps bearing the head of the English King have been burnt in large quantities to signal the destruction of British Imperialism. Monuments, like that of Queen Victoria in Bombay, which are visible symbols of India's slavery, have been demolished by the public. Not less interesting than the above is the attack of transport and communication with a view to dislocating the administration of the country. Tramcar, bus and railway services have been interfered with at places—and the public, when fired on by the police, have, in retaliation, attacked railway stations and damaged railway lines. Attempts have also been made to interrupt postal, telegraph and telephone communications, as a result of which the British authorities have announced that, if in future telegraph and telephone wires are cut, the people of the locality will be punished with death. Last but not least, when subjected to extreme provocations, through brutal attack with batons, rifles, tear-gas, tanks, armoured cars and other weapons, the people have set fire to police stations and destroyed Government property—including food stores reserved for the military. The most tragic feature, however, of this great clash between an unarmed people and a ruthless alien Empire is that, as against tanks, armoured cars and bombs dropped from aeroplanes, the population can find only stones and soda-water bottles to fight with.

The clarion-call of liberty has also reached the Indian soldiers now fighting in Egypt under the British flag. Some of them have laid down their arms, refusing to fight for Britain—while others have actually turned their weapons against the alien oppressors, and during the skirmish that has followed, one British General has been killed. In order to avenge themselves for this incident, the British have, in their rage, shot one man in every 20 in several Indian regiments.

It is absolutely clear that the British authorities are determined to resort to all forms of brutality in order to crush this national revolt. For them, Indian lives are cheap and they are, therefore, freely indulging in shooting, in spite of the fact that the Indian people are quite unarmed and defenseless. Information that has reached me up till now, shows that in India the casualties have amounted to about 700 killed and 4500 wounded. Women have not been spared and they have been thrown into prison in large numbers. Nevertheless, the spirit of the people remains indomitable and irrepressible. What is most encouraging and inspiring in the whole situation is that the campaign is spreading like wild fire from one part of the country to the other—and from the cities into the remote villages. Every action of the people has been drawn into the struggle—the middle-classes, the petty shopkeepers, the factory-workers and the students. And the day is not far off, when the mass of the peasantry will also swing into the national struggle. Friends! When you are in the thick of the fight, you will certainly feel encouraged to hear that Indian news is today on the front page of the world-press and Indian reports are one of the most interesting items in radio-broadcasts all over the world. Every small incident that takes place in the remotest corner of India is immediately flashed to all corners sof the globe, so that everybody is fully informed of the detailed happenings in India from day to day and from hour to hour.

It is also gratifying to know that in this fight with British Imperialism, India does not stand alone. All the powers of the world that are now fighting Britain, are arrayed on the side of India, and in spite of all the maneuvers of Anglo-American propaganda, public opinion throughout the world sympathises with us in our struggle. The more we suffer, the more we sacrifice, and the more we fight, the more sympathy and respect do we earn from abroad—and the more do Indians, all over the world, hold up their heads with dignity and pride.

Let me also assure you that not only is public opinion all over the world on our side but Indians abroad are now wide awake. They are doing their utmost to utilise the present world-situation and to advance the cause of India in every possible way. Indians in the Far East, in America, in Europe and in Africa have already demonstrated their solidarity with you in this struggle and have held meetings and demonstrations everywhere for this purpose. If at any time you want any help from abroad, you have only to ask for it. Your countrymen abroad will then rush to you with all the assistance you may need, and may ask for.

During the last two decades I have been through every phase of our national struggle—from 1921 till 1940. I naturally feel unhappy that today I am not at home to participate in this last campaign. But it will not be long before I am at your side again. Meanwhile, standing outside the clutches of British Imperialism, it will be my duty to fully utilise the international situation for the achievement of India's Independence, to keep the outside world informed of all the facts and of the Indian situation, and so secure from the enemies of Britain, all the sympathy and help that India may now need.

In view of the experience that I have gained from the campaign between 1921 and 1940 and in the light of the present world situation. I may offer the following advice to you, which I believe will ensure our success in this struggle.

Firstly, develop the struggle gradually and expand it all over the country by stages.

Secondly, in planning any action, avoid doing harm to the public as far as possible. Let your aim be to damage the machinery of administration only.

Thirdly, your campaign should now be converted into a guerilla-war without arms. This guerilla-war should have two aims—to destroy Britain's war-production in India and to paralyse the British administration of India.

Fourthly, listen to the broadcasts of Col. Britton in the European service of the B.B.C. and apply Col. Britton's tactics to the Indian situation.

Fifthly, for the general public the following activities are advisable:

(A) Carry on complete boycott of British goods.
(B) Hold public meetings in defiance of the official ban.
(C) All over the country, organise marches to the houses of high Government officials—from the Viceroy downwards. If you happen to meet them demand that they, and their Government, should quit India at once.
(D) Organise processions for entering and occupying Government institutions—like law-courts, secretariat buildings etc., with a view to rendering all work impossible there.

(E) Disobey all laws, if such disobedience will help to embarrass the administration.
(F) Carry on a social boycott of such Indian officials as are really pro-British.
(G) Carry on a social boycott of all Britishers in the country.
(H) Stop paying taxes, provided such non-payment does not bring too much trouble on yourselves.
(I) Begin erecting barricades in streets where there is a likelihood of attack from the police and the military.
(J) Arrange to punish British police officers and prison-officials who show special zeal in oppressing the people.

Sixthly, workers in factories, specially in war factories, should go on strike. If that is not possible they should carry on a go-slow campaign in the factories. They should also carry on small acts of sabotage, i.e. removing nuts and bolts, reducing the steam pressure etc.—if that would dislocate the work, without bringing too much trouble on the workers themselves.

Seventhly, the peasants should immediately stop paying all taxes and rates which help the British Government—provided such nonpayment does not bring too much trouble on themselves.

Eighthly, students should leave their studies and organise guerilla bands for carrying on sabotage. They should, every day, invent new ways of annoying the British authorities and dislocating the administration, e.g. going to members of the Viceroy's Executive Council and demanding their resignation.

Ninthly, women, and specially girl students, should come forward to act as secret messengers and underground workers and to provide shelter for the men who fight.

Tenthly, clerks in Government offices and in war industries should work slowly and inefficiently and should give as much trouble to their masters as possible.

Eleventhly, businessmen should give up doing business with English firms.

Twelfthly, Government officials who are prepared to secretly help the cause, need not resign now.

Thirteenthly, servants working for Englishmen should be organised to go on strike on some pretext or other—i.e. demanding double the present wages. They should be instructed to cook bad food or to mix undesirable things with food and drink—so that living in India will be impossible for Englishmen. Similarly, it should be made impossible for Englishmen to appear in public.

Fourteenthly, all visible symbols of British Imperialism should be destroyed wherever possible—e.g. stamps, monuments, British flags, etc.

Fifteenthly, every attempt should be made to interfere with telegraph, telephone and postal services. Similarly, transport—that is, tram, bus or railway services—should be interrupted—specially when troops are transferred or war-materials are conveyed from one place to another. In arranging this type of sabotage, the public should not be unnecessarily inconvenienced.

In conclusion, I would like to point out that this campaign should be carried on for weeks and months. Activities should be shifted from place to place if necessary, in order to avoid being crushed. If this guerilla-war is continued sufficiently long then freedom will come, when British Imperialism ultimately is brought down, as the cumulative effect of the defeats on different fronts in different parts of the world.

Friends! There is no need to be depressed, because the leaders have all been thrown into prison. On the contrary, their incarceration should serve as a perpetual inspiration to the entire nation. Have we not been trained during the last 20 years to prosecute a campaign even when all the leading men are in person. The leaders who have been taken away from you have left behind the plan of action. That plan has to be fulfilled by you, regardless of consequences. You have to fight on every front and by all possible means, so that the British administration of India may be thrown out of gear and then overthrown.

I have no doubt, Friends, that you realise that India's battle is being fought, not in India alone, but throughout this wide world—on every battle-field, where history is now being made. All the forces that are today fighting to destroy this accursed Empire are fighting not for themselves alone—but incidentally for India as well. Nevertheless, the main brunt of the task of liberating India has to be borne by the Indian people themselves. Therefore, it will be your task to carry on the struggle to a victorious conclusion, no matter what the suffering or sacrifice may be. Freedom cannot be won without shedding the blood of martyrs. And even if freedom could be won without paying that price, it would not be worth having. It is the baptism of blood, which gives a nation the strength to achieve liberty and to preserve it.

The whole world now sees that the velvet glove which ordinarily hides the mailed fist of Britain has now been cast away and brute force—naked and unashamed—rules over India. Behind the thick screen of gas, underneath the heavy blows of police batons, amid the continual whistle of bullets and the angry defiance of the injured and dying—the soul of India asks—'Where are the four freedoms?' The words float over the seven seas to all corners of the globe—but Washington does not reply. After a pause, the soul of India asks again—'Where is the Atlantic Charter which guaranteed to every nation its own Government?' This time Downing Street and White House reply simultaneously—'That Charter was not meant for India.'

This is the British Imperialism which the Indian people have known so well—ever since 1857, when innocent and unarmed people were blown up into the air with the help of cannon. This is the British Imperialism, which in its Indian policy, has the fullest support, not only of the Conservative and Liberal parties, but also of the Labour Party. Today, that Imperialism—hand-in-glove with Yankee Imperialism—stands unmasked before the world. But India has nothing to fear. Through persecution and tortures, her soul has been roused and through terror and brutality will she march towards her goal.

Friends! At a time when the modern weapons of massacre have been let loose on you and Imperialist brutality is running riot—do not forget for one moment that the British Empire is now on its last legs. Can you expect that the Imperialist brutes will throw up the sponge before they have struck their last blows? No, friends—be prepared that the apostles of freedom and democracy and the authors of the Atlantic Charter will do their very worst in the days to come. But that does not matter. Before dawn comes the darkest hour. Therefore, muster all your strength and courage in this fateful hour. Sisters and brothers! Be brave and continue the struggle, for freedom is at hand. Let your slogans be—'Now or Never'—Victory or Death!'

29

Join India's Epic Struggle

BROADCAST, 31 AUGUST 1942[1]

This is Subhas Chandra Bose speaking to you over the Azad Hind Radio.

Comrades! Since I spoke to you last, about two weeks ago, the movement in India has been continuing with unabated vigour, and has been spreading like wildfire from the towns to the countryside. The British propaganda machinery throughout the month has tried to give the impression that the campaign is now subsiding and things are quietening down. But this attempt has completely failed, because in the same breath the B.B.C. and its agents have given, or rather have been forced to give, news of more shooting on unarmed men and women all over the country. I can assure you that in the year of grace 1942, India can no longer be isolated from the rest of the world, however much Britain may try to draw a veil over that land. As a matter of fact, every bit of news regarding India's national struggle, every incident in Indian towns and villages, every case of shooting, whether in Ramnath or in Wardha, in Bikrampore or in Lucknow, is immediately flashed over the world, is broadcast over the radio and published in the Press in all those countries that are either hostile to the Allied Powers or are neutral. Comrades, I know very well how in all the previous campaigns we were hard put to inform the outside world about the happenings in India and about the atrocities committed by British imperialists. Today, the problem does not exist, and it is my pleasant task to keep the outside world informed about all events in India and to secure all the sympathy and help that India may need in her hour of trial. If today you could see with your own eyes and hear with your own ears all that is being

---

[1] Broadcast over Azad Hind Radio (Germany) on 31 August 1942.

propagated by your friends abroad about India's epic struggle, you would realise the measure of sympathy that India is receiving from the enemies of British imperialism. And, this sympathy for India is bound to grow in volume and intensity as British terror and brutality increases. The more we suffer and the more we sacrifice in the pursuit of our national freedom, the more will India's prestige go up in the eyes of the world.

Comrades, I should like to tell you further that while we have gained the moral sympathies of public opinion throughout the world, it is also possible for us to obtain from abroad any help that we may need for our emancipation. Therefore in the fight against all the modern forms of terror and brutality, if you feel overwhelmed at any time and if you desire your friends abroad to give you the hand of assistance, you have only to say so. But these friends who are anxious to see India free, will not offer their help to you, so long as you do not need it, and for our national honour and self-interest, we should not ask for any assistance so long as we can do without it. In this connection I would appeal to you once again, to fully trust your countrymen abroad who are working heart and soul with you for the speedy liberation of India. We are today the custodians of India's national honour, the 'unofficial ambassadors' of free India. As at home, so also abroad, we stand always for Independence, and we shall never permit vital encroachments on our national sovereignty by any foreign power. Do not be carried away by ideological considerations; do not bother about the internal politics of other countries, which is no concern of ours. Believe me when I say that the enemies of British imperialism are our friends and allies. It is to their interest to see the British Empire broken up, and India is once again free. And they know very well that so long as India remains under the British yoke, there can be no victory for them and there can be no peace. In the political field, I should be the last man to expect foreign Powers to sympathise with us if it were not in their interest to do so.

Comrades, you must have observed how during the last few months the British Empire has been passing through its darkest hours. Gone are the days when London was the metropolis of the World. Gone are the days when kings and statesmen had to wend their way to London in order to have their problems solved. Gone are the days when the American President had to come to Europe to meet the British Prime Minister. As the English poet, Tennyson, has himself said, 'The old order changeth yielding place to the new, and God fulfils himself in many ways.' Consequently, the British Prime Minister has now to run to New York and Washington and Americans in Britain are declared to be outside the jurisdiction of British laws, and American officers have refused command of British forces in many theatres of war. Thus Britain and her Empire are fast becoming a colony of Roosevelt's 'New Empire'. But India has no desire to remain in the Old Empire, and she must, therefore, now fight both the old imperialism as well as the new. The most interesting phase of the metamorphosis that has overtaken the British Empire is the fact that the High Priest of Imperialism, the arch-enemy of Indian Nationalism, the sworn opponent of all forms of Socialism, the British Prime Minister, Winston Churchill, has had to swallow all his former imperialist pride and present himself at the gates of the Kremlin in Moscow.

Is it not significant that in his desperation this representative of British imperialism should do everything else, but under no circumstances will he think of recognising India's independence? India is the jewel of the British Empire and in order to do everything possible to keep this jewel, the British people will fight to the last. The Indian people, therefore, and particularly the leaders, should banish all hopes that Britain will accede to India's demands, and should carry on the struggle till the last Britisher is expelled from India. In the last days of our campaign there will be much suffering and sorrow, much persecution and slaughter, much suppression and massacre. But that is the price of liberty and it has to be paid. It is but natural that in its last hours the British lion will bite hard, but it is after all the bite of a dying lion, and we shall survive it.

Comrades, in this critical hour our strategy should consist in continuing the fight for our independence regardless of the consequences. The British Empire will soon collapse and break up as a result of shattering defeats in all the theatres of war. As the final dismemberment of the Empire takes place powers will automatically come into the hands of the Indian people. Our final victory will come as a result of our efforts alone. Consequently, it does not matter in the least if we in India suffer temporary setbacks, specially when we are confronted with machine-guns, bombs, tanks and aeroplanes. Our task is to continue the national struggle in spite of all obstacles and setbacks till the hour of liberation arrives.

There is no cause to be depressed because the leaders are imprisoned. On the contrary, their sufferings will serve as a perpetual inspiration to the entire nation. I have been offering during the last 20 years to conduct the campaign even when all the men are in prison. Moreover, those who are now away from the field of action have given you the plan that has to be executed by you now.

Comrades, I have already assured you that whatever I have been doing abroad is in accordance with the wishes of a very large section of my countrymen. I will not do anything which the whole of India will not wholeheartedly endorse. Ever since I left home I have remained in intimate contact with my countrymen at home through more channels than one, in spite of all the efforts of the Intelligence Bureau of the Government of India and the British Secret Service. During the last few months you have had proof of my close contact with my countrymen in India and many of you know by now how you can communicate with me whenever you so desire. I may now tell you that it is no longer possible for the British to prevent my going to India or getting out whenever I wish to do so. I have seen some of the secret reports of the Government of India regarding the 'Azad Hind Radio' and myself, and they have made me laugh. The British authorities think that they know all about me, but I shall one day be able to give them the fight of their lives. There is no harm if I also inform the British Government in this connection that the tactics they have been using in enemy countries have been carefully studied by our men, and they have been found to be extremely useful in our fight against our old enemy, British imperialism.

Comrades, at the present moment all the countries that are being suppressed or dominated by Britain are either in a state of revolt or are preparing for one. If we in India continue our struggle we shall not only effect our emancipation speedily, but will also expedite the liberation of all countries exploited and dominated by Britain. On the other hand, if the Indian people remain inactive, the enemies of Britain will take the initiative in expelling the British from India. The British Empire is in any case doomed, and the only question is as to what will happen to us when its final dissolution takes place. Shall we obtain our freedom as a right from other Powers or shall we win it by our own effort? I would request Mr Jinnah, Mr Savarkar and all those leaders who still think of a compromise with the British to realise once for all that in the world of tomorrow there will be no British Empire. All these individuals, groups or parties who now participate in the fight for freedom will have an honoured place in the India of tomorrow. The supporters of British imperialism will naturally become non-entities in a free India. In this connection I will appeal earnestly to all parties and groups to consider this and to think in terms of nationalism and anti-imperialism, and to come forward and join the epic struggle that is going on now. I appeal to the progressive elements of the Muslim League, with some of whom I have had the privilege of cooperating in the work of the Calcutta Corporation in 1940. I appeal to the brave 'Majlis-i-Ahrar', the nationalist Muslim Party of India, that started the Civil Disobedience campaign in 1939 against Britain's war effort before any other party did so. I appeal to the 'Jamiat-ul-Ulema', the old representative organisation of the Ulemas or the Muslim divines of India, led by that distinguished patriot and leader Mufti Khifayat Ullah. I appeal to the Azad (Independent) Muslim League, another important organisation of the nationalist Muslims of India. I appeal to the 'Akali Dal', the leading nationalist Sikh party of India. And last but not least I appeal to the 'Praja Party' of Bengal, which commands the confidence of that province, and is led by well-known patriots. I have no doubt that if all these organisations join in this struggle the day of India's liberation will be drawn nearer.

The campaign that is now going on in India may be described as a non-violent guerrilla warfare. In this guerrilla war the tactics of dispersal have to be employed. In other words, we should spread out our activities all over the country so that the British police and military may not be able to concentrate their attack on one point. In accordance with the principles of guerrilla war, we should also be as mobile as possible and should move continuously from place to place. The authorities should never be able to predict where our activities will emerge next. Friends, as you know already, I have been through all the campaigns between 1921 and 1940, and I know the causes of their failure. I have now had the opportunity of taking expert advice with regard to the tactics of guerrilla warfare, and I am in a position to offer you some suggestions as to how this present campaign should be brought to a victorious end. The object of this non-violent guerrilla campaign should be a two-fold one. Firstly, to destroy war production in India, and secondly, to paralyse the British administration in that country. Keeping this object in view, every section of the community should participate in the struggle. Firstly, stop paying all taxes that directly or indirectly bring revenue to the Government. Secondly, workers in all industries should either launch a 'stay-in' strike or try to hamper production by conducting a 'go-slow' campaign inside the factories. They should also carry out sabotage with such methods as removing of nuts and bolts in order to impede production. Thirdly, students should organise secret guerrilla bands for carrying on sabotage in different parts of the country. They should also invent new ways of annoying the British authorities, for example, burning stamps, etc., in post offices, destroying British monuments, etc. Fourthly, women, and especially girl students, should do underground work of all kinds especially as secret messengers or to provide shelter for the men who fight. Fifthly, Government officials, who are prepared to help the campaign, should not resign their posts but those in Government offices and in war industries should give all available information to fighters outside and should try to hamper production by working inefficiently. Sixthly, servants, who are working in the houses of Britishers, should be organised for the purpose of giving trouble to their masters, for example by demanding higher salaries, cooking and serving bad food and drinks, etc. Seventhly, Indians should give up all business with banks, firms, insurance companies, etc. Eighthly, listen to the broadcasts of Col. Britton in the European Service of the B.B.C. and apply the Colonel's tactics to the Indian situation.

For the general public I also suggest the following activities:

(a) Boycott of British goods, including burning of British stalls and Government stores.
(b) Total boycott of all Britishers in India and of those Indians who are pro-British.
(c) Holding of public meetings and demonstrations in spite of official prohibition.
(d) Publishing of secret bulletins and setting up of secret radio station.
(e) Marching to the houses of British Government officials and demanding their departure from India.

(f) Organising of processions for entering and occupying Government offices, Secretarial buildings, Law courts etc. with a view to hampering the administration.
(g) Arranging to punish police officers and prison officials who oppress and persecute the people.
(h) Begin erecting barricades in the streets where there is a likelihood of attack from the police and the military.
(i) Setting fire to Government offices and factories which are working for war purposes.
(j) Interrupting postal, telegraph and telephone communication as frequently as possible and in different places.
(k) Interrupting railway, bus and tram services whenever there is a possibility of hampering the transport of soldiers or of war material.
(l) Destroying police stations, railway stations and jails in isolated places.

Comrades I can assure you, that as soon as this programme is put into operation, the administrative machinery can be brought to a standstill. In this connection, I must remind you that in a non-violent guerrilla campaign the peasantry always plays a decisive part. I am glad to observe that in several provinces—in Bihar and in the Central Provinces—*the peasants are already in the forefront.* I earnestly hope that Swami Sahajanand Saraswati and other peasant leaders, who together with the 'Forward Bloc' started the fight long before Mahatma Gandhi, will now lead the campaign to a victorious conclusion. I will appeal to Swami Sahajanand and the leaders of the Kisan (Peasant) Movement to come forward and fulfil their leading role in the last phase of the fight. We want Swaraj for the masses, Swaraj for the workers and the peasants. It is therefore the duty of the workers and the peasants to emerge as the vanguard of the national army at the time when the future of India is being made. It is the law of nature that those who fight for liberty and win it, will retain power and responsibility. It is very encouraging, friends, to find that the people of Indian States have began to participate in this All-India struggle. Reports to the effect have already come from Baroda, Mysore and Hyderabad, and I am confident that the day is not far off when the States people will line up with the people of British India and form a common front against the combined friends of British imperialism and the Indian Princes. Most gratifying of all is the news that the clarion call of liberty has reached the ears and the hearts of our soldiers at home and abroad. They have no doubt been court-martialled with characteristic British brutality. But the fire is spreading from one place to another. A large number of soldiers have voluntarily deserted to join the Axis forces in Egypt and they are being welcomed with open arms by them. All the Indian fighting units have been withdrawn from the El Alamein front, as being unreliable. No wonder some supporters of British imperialism have been brought up from India in order to impress the Indian troops. But their efforts have so far failed. I will be able to keep the outside world informed of all the facts of the Indian situation so to secure from the enemies of Britain all the help that India may now need.

In this connection I would like to point out that this campaign should be carried out for weeks and if necessary for months. If this non-violent guerilla war should continue sufficiently long, freedom will come because British imperialism will ultimately break down owing to the cumulative effect of defeats sustained on different fronts. Do not forget for one moment that the British Empire is now on its last legs.

At the same time be prepared for every suffering because the apostles of freedom and democracy and the authors of the Atlantic Charter may do their very worst in the days to come. Before dawn comes the darkest hour. Be brave and continue the struggle, for freedom is at hand. Let your slogan be 'Now or Never'; 'Victory or Death'; 'Inquilab Zindabad'.

30

Free India and Her Problems

AUGUST 1942[1]

The New Awakening

The British occupation of India began in 1757 when one province—namely Bengal—first passed into the hands of the British. The occupation was extended by stages and was finally completed in 1858, after the failure of the great revolution of 1857. This revolution is described by the English historian as 'Sepoy Mutiny,' but is regarded by the Indian people as the 'First War of Independence.' In the early stages the revolution was very successful, but it failed at the end, owing to certain defects in strategy and in diplomacy, on the part of the Indian leaders. On the British side, both strategy and diplomacy were superior. Nevertheless the British could win only with the greatest difficulty.

After the failure of the revolution there was a reign of terror throughout the country. The Indian people were thoroughly disarmed and they continue disarmed up to the present day. They now realise that they committed the greatest blunder in their history by submitting to disarmament in 1858, because disarmament weakened and emasculated the nation to a large extent. After the failure of the revolution of 1857, the Indian people were depressed for a time. Then, in 1885, with the birth of the Indian National Congress began the political awakening—which was stimulated by revolutions in other parts of the world. With the beginning of the present century, the nationalist movement developed two methods, economic boycott of British goods and secret insurrection. In 1920, after the last world war, Gandhi

[1] Published in German in 'Wille and Macht' (August 1942) and reprinted in *Azad Hind* (9/10, 1942).

introduced the new method of mass civil disobedience, or passive resistance, the object of which was the overthrow of the foreign administration even without arms. All these developments have now brought India to a stage when it is possible for the Indian people to throw out the British from India.

The Situation Today

The situation in India today is such that the British are hated by everybody. But while the vast majority of the people want to utilise the present international crisis for overthrowing the British yoke, a section of the population does not feel strong enough to do so and therefore wants to come to a compromise with the British Government, with a view to getting what is possible out of them. There is no Indian who cooperates with the British out of moral conviction. Hence British rule does not rest on the goodwill of the Indian people but only on British bayonets.

Many people cannot understand how the British can dominate such a big country like India with a comparatively small army. The secret however, is that with a small but modern army, it is possible to suppress a vast but unarmed population. So long as this modern army of occupation is not involved in a war with another power, it can put down by sheer brute-force any internal upheaval organised by the people. But now that the British are engaged in a war with other powers and have been considerably weakened thereby, it has become possible for the Indian people to work up a revolution which will end British rule once for all. But it is necessary for the Indian people to take up arms in their struggle and to cooperate with those powers that are fighting Britain today. This task, Gandhi will not accomplish—hence India now needs a new leadership.

When India is Free

A question which many people ask is as to what will happen when the British are forced to leave India. British propaganda has made many people think that without the British there will be anarchy and chaos in India. These people conveniently forget that British occupation began only in 1757 and was not complete till 1857—while India is a land whose history is measured by thousands of years. If culture, civilisation, administration and economic prosperity were possible in India before British rule—they will also be possible after British rule. In fact, under British rule, the culture and civilisation of India has been suppressed, the administration has been denationalised and a land that was formerly rich and prosperous has become one of the poorest in the world.

A New Civil Administration

When the British are expelled from India, the first task will be to set up a new Government and establish order and public security. A new Government will necessarily imply the reorganisation of the civil administration and the creation of a national army. Reorganising the civil administration will be a comparatively easy task. In the past, the civil administration has always been run by the Indians and only on the top, have there been Britishers. But during the last twenty years, Indians have been gradually replacing Britishers in the highest positions. In the central Government, the members of he Viceroy's Cabinet have been partly Indians. In the provincial Governments, since 1937, the Ministers have been all Indians and English officials have worked under them. In the highest positions wherever Indians have replaced Britishers, they have proved more capable than the latter. Indian Ministers and Indian officials know the country much better and are more interested in its welfare than Britishers. It is, therefore, natural that they should work more efficiently than Britishers have done in the past. In short, we have such a trained and experienced body of Indian officials today that reorganising the civil administration will not be at all difficult. The new Government of Free India will only have to lay down a new policy and a new progranmme and furnish a new leadership at the top, for the civil administration.

A National Army

Building up a national army will be a more difficult task. India has, of course, a large number of trained and experienced soldiers and their number has been augmented as a result of the present war. But till quite recently, the Indian army was officered largely by Britishers, and in the higher ranks, the officers were exclusively Britishers. Owing to war conditions, the British have now been forced to appoint a large number of Indian officers and the higher ranks have also been opened to a few Indians. Modern weapons, like tanks, aeroplanes, heavy artillery, etc. which were formerly reserved for Britishers, have, under the pressure of circumstances, also been handed over to Indians. Nevertheless, the dearth of Indian officers of high rank remains and will present some difficulty in building up a national army. In this connection, India's chief problem will be to train up a large number of officers of all ranks within in a short period—say ten years—and thereby complete the formation of National Army. Along with the Army, a Navy and an Air Force will also have to be built up and all this work will have to be speeded up as much as possible. If India can enjoy peace for some time and the assistance of some friendly powers be forthcoming, then the problem of organising national defence can be satisfactory solved.

The New State

It would be wrong to dogmatise from now about the exact form of the future Indian state. One can only indicate the principles, which will underlie that state and determine its form. India has had experience of several Empires in the past and this experience will furnish the background on which we shall have to build in future. Then we shall have to consider the causes which led to our political downfall and prevent their recurrence in future. Further, we shall have to remember that the intelligentsia of India today is quite familiar with modern political institutions and is greatly interested in them. We shall also have to consider the political experiments made in different parts of Europe in the post-Versailles period. And lastly, we shall have to consider the requirements of the Indian situation.

One thing, however, is clear. There will be a strong Central Government. Without such a Government, order and public security cannot be safeguarded. Behind this Government will stand a well-organised, disciplined all-India party, which will be the chief instrument for maintaining national unity.

The state will guarantee complete religious and cultural freedom for individuals and groups and there will be no state-religion. In the matter of political and economic rights there will be perfect equality among the whole population. When every individual has employment, food and education and has freedom in religious and cultural matters, there will be no more minorities problem in India.

When the new regime is established and the state-machinery begins to function smoothly, power will be decentralised and the provincial governments will be given more responsibility.

National Unity

The state will have to do everything possible to unify the whole nation and all methods of propaganda—press, radio, cinema, theatre, etc.—will have to be utilised for this purpose. All anti-national and disruptive elements will have to be firmly suppressed along with such secret British agents as may still exist in the country. An adequate police force will have to be organised for this purpose and the law will have to be amended, so that offences against national unity may be punished heavily. Hindustani, which is already understood in most parts of the country, will be adopted as the common language for India. Special emphasis will have to be laid on the proper education of boys and girls and of students in the schools and in the universities, so that they may imbibe the spirit of national unity at an early age.

British propaganda has deliberately created the impression that the Indian Mohammedans are against the Independence movement. But this is altogether false. The fact is that in the nationalist movement, there is a large percentage of Mohammedans. The President of the Indian National Congress today is Azad—a Mohammedan. The vast majority of the Indian Mohammedans are anti-British and want to see India free. There is no doubt that pro-British parties among both Mohammedans and Hindus are organised as religious parties. But they should not be regarded as representing the people.

The great revolution of 1857 was a grand example of national unity. The war was fought under the flag of Bahadur Shah, a Mohammedan, and all sections of the people joined in it. Since then Indian Mohammedans have continued to work for national freedom. Indian Mohammedans are as much children of the soil as the rest of the Indian population and their interests are identical. The Mohammedan (or Muslim) problem in India today is an artificial creation of the British similar to the Ulster-problem in Ireland and the Jewish problem in Palestine. It will disappear when British rule is swept away.

Social Problems

When the new regime is established, India will be able to concentrate her whole attention on the solution of the social problems. The most important social problem is that of poverty and unemployment. India's poverty under British rule has been due principally to two causes—systematic destruction of Indian industries by the British Government and lack of scientific agriculture. In pre-British days, India produced all her requirements in food and industry and she exported her surplus industrial products to Europe, e.g. textile goods. The advent of the industrial revolution and political domination by Britain destroyed the old industrial structure of India and she was not allowed to build up a new one. Britain purposely kept India in the position of a supplier of raw materials for British industries. The result was that millions of Indians who formerly lived on industry were thrown out of employment. Foreign rule has impoverished the peasantry and has prevented the introduction of modern scientific agriculture. The result of this has been that the once rich soil of India has a very poor yield and can no longer feed the peasant. About 70 per cent of the peasantry have no work for about six months in the year. India will therefore need industrialisation and scientific agriculture through state aid, if she has to solve the problem of poverty and unemployment.

Under foreign rule, the Britisher was not only the ruler, but also the employer of labour. Hence labour has been kept in a wretched condition. The Free Indian State will have to look after the welfare of the labourer, providing him with a living wage, sickness insurance, compensation for accident, etc. Similarly, the peasant will have to be given relief from excessive taxation and also from his appalling indebtedness. In this connection, institutions for the welfare of labour, like 'Arbeitsdienst', 'Winterhilfe', 'Kraft durch Freude', etc. will be of great interest to India. Next in importance is the problem of public health. This has also remained unsolved under British rule. Fortunately India now has a large number of qualified doctors who are even superior to the English doctors available in India and who are well acquainted with questions of public health. Given state-support and sufficient financial help, they can launch a gigantic effort for eradication of disease. India's ancient systems of medicine, Ayurveda and Unani, can also be helpful in this connection.

Then we have the terrific problem of illiteracy, the percentage of which is about 90 per cent in many parts of the country. But this problem is not at all difficult to tackle, if the state can provide the necessary funds. We have now a large number of educated men and women, who are without employment. Under Free India, all these men and women could be sent to work at once all over the country in order to erect schools, colleges and universities. Side by side with this work, experiments will have to be made for evolving a national system of education in accordance with the needs of the Indian people. Fortunately, experiments are already being made in several places in this connection, e.g. at Tagore's school, Santiniketan, at the Gurukul institution at Hardvar, at the Hindu University of Benares, at Jamia-Milia (National Muslim) University at Delhi, at Gandhi's School near Wardha, etc. Moreover, there are the educational institutions which have been handed down to us from pre-British days which are also interesting.

Regarding the future script for India, my own view is that without forcibly abolishing the scripts now prevalent in the country, the Free India Government should encourage and popularise the Latin script.

Finance

The problem as to how Free India will get the money required for her big schemes is an important one. Britain has robbed India of her gold and silver and what little still remains, will certainly be removed, before the British leave the country. India's national economy will, naturally, have to discard the Gold Standard and accept the doctrine that national wealth depends on Labour and production and not on gold. Foreign trade will have to be brought under state control and organised on the principle of barter (exchange of goods) as Germany has done since 1933.

Planning Committee

While dealing with the problems of reconstruction, it would be interesting to know that in December 1938, when I was the President of the Indian National Congress, I inaugurated a National Planning Committee, for drawing up plans for reconstruction in every department of life. This Committee has already done valuable work and its reports will be helpful for our future activity.

The Princes

The Indian Princes and their States are an anachronism which must soon be abolished. They would have disappeared long ago if the British had not preserved them in order to hamper the unification of the country. Most of the Princes are active supporters of the British Government and there is not a single Prince who is likely to play a role similar to that which Piedmont played in the Risorgimento movement in Italy. Among the people of the States who are one-fourth of the total Indian population, there is a popular movement, which is closely connected with the Congress movement in British India. The Princes will naturally disappear along with the British rule since most of them are very unpopular with their own people. But they cannot present any difficulty to the Free India Government, as the British Government has not allowed any prince to have a modern Army. Contrary to expectation, if the princes were to join the revolution, one would naturally come to a settlement with them.

International Relations

In the past, one of the causes of India's downfall has been her isolation from the outside world. In future, India must, therefore, remain in intimate contact with other nations. Geographically, India has a position between the East and the West, which will probably conform to her cultural, economic and political role. It is but natural that in future India should have the closest relations with the Tripartite Powers who are now fighting India's enemy.

India will need help from abroad for her speedy industrialisation as well as for the organisation of her Army, Navy and Air Force. She will, therefore, require machinery of all kinds, scientific and technical knowledge and equipment, and scientific and technical experts. She will also require military experts and military equipment for building up her national defence. In these matters, the Tripartite Powers can render valuable assistance. In Free India, the standard of living will rise rapidly and, in consequence thereof, consumption will increase by leaps and bounds. Free India will thereby become one of the biggest markets for manufactured goods. This should be of interest to all industrially advanced countries.

In return, India could contribute something to the common culture and civilisation of humanity. In religion and philosophy, in architecture, in painting, dancing and music and in other arts and handicrafts, India could offer something unique to the world. And judging from the progress made, despite the handicaps of foreign rule, I feel sure that very soon India will be able to achieve much in scientific research and industrial development.

Young India has a gigantic task to fulfil. There are tremendous difficulties to overcome, no doubt, but there is also the joy and glory of struggle and ultimate victory.

31

India and Germany

SPEECH, 11 SEPTEMBER 1942[1]

Herr Reichssstatthalter—Obergruppenführer Lorenz
Herr Burgermeister, and Gentlemen!

I am profoundly thankful to you for the warm and cordial welcome which my countrymen and myself have received today at your hands on the occasion of our visit to your historic city. In the history of Germany and indeed of Europe—Hamburg occupies a unique position and our meeting here on this occasion has, therefore, a special significance.

I am exceedingly grateful, also, for the kind and friendly words spoken here this evening about our dear country. We are today engaged in a life-and-death struggle with a very powerful Empire and any sympathy that we may receive now will naturally have great value and importance for us than if we had been living under normal circumstances.

Herr Burgermeister, we have assembled here today at your invitation for performing the foundation ceremony of the Deutsch-Indische Gesellschaft in Hamburg. It will, therefore, be in the fitness of things if I say a few words about the attitude of the Indian people towards your great country.

We know very well that there was a time when, at the beginning of the modern era in history, several European powers were competing among themselves for gaining a foothold in India. Just at that moment, India was passing through an internal crisis and was therefore weak in her opposition to these foreign powers. But it is noteworthy that at that time Germany was not among those powers that had evil intentions about India. In fact, Germany's approach to India was, from the very

---

[1] Speech delivered on the occasion of the foundation of the Indo-German Society in Hamburg, 11 September 1942 and printed in *Azad Hind* (7/8, 1942).

beginning, entirely intellectual, moral and spiritual. When the British succeeded in dominating our country, they tried their level best to paint everything Indian as of inferior quality. At that psychological moment, when India needed some moral help, German scholars, thinkers and savants discovered India and Indian culture. This is a fact which we can never forget, and it is this cultural bond, devoid of all selfish and material interest, which has remained the basis of German-Indian relations up to the present day.

Some of the foremost poets and thinkers of Germany, like Goethe, Schopenhauer, Ruckert and Schlegel, were the first Europeans to express their appreciation of Indian culture. Schopenhauer expressed his admiration of Indian philosophy as embodied in the Upanishads and in Buddhism—while Goethe gave utterance to his enthusiasm for Indian literature and drama. Goethe wrote for instance:

> Would'st thou the young year's blossoms
> and the fruits of its decline.
> And all by which the soul is charmed,
> enraptured, feasted, fed?
> Would'st thou the earth and heaven itself
> In thine sole name combine?
> I name thee, O Sakuntala,
> And all at once is said.

The work begun by Goethe, Schopenhauer, Schlegel and others, was continued by a host of scholars and writers, including Max Muller and Deussen, who developed the German-Indian relations still further. A number of German scholars also went to India and made social contacts with the Indian people and particularly with the intellectual classes in India. Thus, by 1914, when the last war broke out, the cultural relations between Germany and India were intimate and profound.

The Indian people had followed with deep interest and admiration the rapid growth and development of German thought and culture in the nineteenth century. From a purely cultural interest in Germany—they were gradually attracted by the political development and expansion of the German people. Then there arose the hope and expectation that the new Germany would become a first-class world-power able to challenge and defeat the powerful British Empire. When

India was still not politically fully ripe, the last world-war broke out in 1914. There was a wide-spread hope that Germany would win the war and every German victory was, therefore, acclaimed with enthusiasm by the Indian people. Since India was not yet politically well-organised, the Indian people could not make the fullest use of the opportunity. Nevertheless, a section of the Indian people attempted a revolution in India, which unfortunately did not succeed—and in Germany, a number of Indians worked hand in hand with the German Government from 1914 to 1918.

Besides the cultural and political bonds uniting Germany and India—there were economic bonds as well, which gradually became more and more important. The beginning of the twentieth century saw the birth of the Boycott and Swadeshi movement in India. The aim of the Boycott movement was to eschew British goods altogether, while the aim of the Swadeshi movement was to build up Indian industries on the basis of economic 'autarchy'. Indian youths travelled to Europe and Japan and specially to Germany in order to study modern methods of industrial development and on their return home they began to start new industries. On the German side, the rapid industrialisation of that country demanded new markets all over the world and the industrial circles in Germany, therefore, became interested in the steadily growing Indian market.

It will now be seen that cultural, political and economic factors form the background of German–Indian relations. On the Indian side, these relations have been rendered more intimate and profound, as a result of genuine sympathy for Germany, following the Treaty of Versailles in 1919. This feeling was given expression to by the great Indian poet Rabindranath Tagore, when he visited Germany in 1926.

Since 1933 British agencies have carried on a continuous and intensive propaganda in India against the ideology of National Socialism with a view to creating an anti-Axis feeling in that country. They had some success at first, but the outbreak of the present war in 1939 has revolutionised public opinion in India.

Since 1938 I have consistently propagated the idea that this war means for India a golden opportunity for achieving her independence and that India should line up with the enemies of British Imperialism and fight for her freedom. My party within the Greater Nationalist

Party—the Indian National Congress—can perhaps claim that largely as a result of its efforts, public opinion in India today is so strongly anti-British and the majority of the Indian people are now pro-Axis in their general attitude.

Herr Reichsstatthalter, we are convinced that in this war, Britain will be defeated and her Empire will be broken up. We are also convinced that out of the dissolution of the British Empire India will emerge once again as an independent state. We are, consequently, now engaged in the two-fold task of participating in the fight against Britain and at the same time, in preparing our plans for Free India.

The time is, therefore, opportune for considering India's future international relations and for taking immediate steps to develop them. From the experience of the last 100 years the Indian people have learnt that one of the principal causes of India's downfall was her isolation from the rest of the world. India must therefore develop close contact with the outside world in future—and, in particular, with those powers that are opposed to British Imperialism and are friendly to India. The basis of such contact must naturally be cultural, political and economic.

One of the best methods for developing this contact is to establish societies in Germany and later on in India when the British have been driven out of that country. I am glad that no time is being lost for taking the necessary steps in this direction and I am particularly thankful to Hamburg for taking the initiative in the matter. Hamburg has a long tradition as the most important centre of international trade and commerce in Germany. Moreover, it is, for Germany, the door for the outside world and to the East. It is, therefore, in the fitness of things that Hamburg should be charged with the responsibility of founding the Deustch-Indische Gesselschaft.

Herr Reichsstatthalter, permit me to say that for me, personally, the Deutsch-Indische Gesellschaft signifies the fulfilment of an old idea— of an old dream. Since the year 1933 I have travelled extensively and wherever I have found interest in India, I have endeavoured to found a society for cultivating contact between that country and my own. In the course of these efforts, I was able to assist in the foundation of a similar society in Vienna in 1934. Today it is a very great pleasure and honour for me to assist in the foundation of the Deutsch-Indische Gesellschaft in Hamburg. I have no doubt that Hamburg will afford an inspiration for the foundation of other societies—not only in Germany, but throughout Europe as well. The more links that India can forge with the outside world—the better it will be for her.

In conclusion I heartily thank you once again for the warm hospitality you have extended to my countrymen and to myself and also for all that you have done for the promotion of German–Indian relations. I also thank you heartily, Herr Burgermeister, for kindly making me an honorary member of this Deutsch-Indische Gesellschaft. I may assure you that in your work you can always count on our fullest cooperation. I have no doubt that this work will be greatly conducive to the welfare of our two countries.

Long live Germany!
Long live Free India!

32

The USA, Britain and India

BROADCAST, 15 OCTOBER 1942[1]

This is Subhas Chandra Bose speaking from Berlin.

Countrymen and friends! Since I spoke to you last over the radio, I have been travelling in another part of Europe in order to see conditions with my own eyes, and to establish contacts with my countrymen living there. On my return to Berlin, I have once again accepted the hospitality of the short-wave station here in order to speak to my countrymen all over the world. I desire to put before them the world situation so that all of us may clearly understand and determine our duty in future.

Every Indian, whether at home or abroad, must have realised that since September 1939 the position of India *vis-à-vis* Britain has not undergone any change for the better, no matter what the military situation may have been during this period. There is not a single Indian who believes that if Britain were to win the war by some chance the position of India would improve as a consequence thereof. But I know that there are responsible Indians in high positions who believed at one time that if Britain suffered some serious reverses in the war the British Government would be in a chastened mood and would then contemplate a compromise with India. This expectation has not been fulfilled owing to the fact that the minds of British imperialists, like Churchill and Amery, work in a different way and their political strategy is of a different sort. From the beginning, these imperialists had decided once for all not to surrender one jot to the demand for Indian independence. According to the needs of the situation, they would rather surrender to the United States of America, and later on they would try to make up

---

[1] Broadcast from Berlin on 15 October 1942.

for their losses by exploiting India even more than before. For this reason liberal-democrat politicians like Sir Stafford Cripps, who advocated some sort of an understanding with India, were kicked out of the war Cabinet.

The policy of the ruling classes in the United States of America is now clear to the whole world. There is no hush about it any more. One has only to hear all the utterances of their public men in order to comprehend it. It is claimed by them that this country is in the American zone of influence and all other Powers, including the British, should acknowledge this fact and accordingly. Strangely enough, even among British politicians a school of thought has already grown up which openly declares that Britain's place is a subordinate one, that the British should accept the world hegemony of the United States as an indisputable fact, and that it should merely try to hold together the Empire by some means or other. There can be no surer indication of demoralisation in the British camp than the fact that British politicians have accepted defeat in advance. To the neutral observer, the British Empire presents a tragic spectacle indeed, because it is handing over one part of its territory unwillingly to its enemies and another part voluntarily to its great ally.

President Roosevelt is not committing the mistake which President Wilson did in the last war. Consequently, he is not helping Britain by a supply of war material and economic assistance gratis. His Government is insisting on cash payment everywhere and in consequence British assets and securities all over the world are evaporating into thin air while the Americans are taking control of them. The U.S. Government has been occupying military bases all over the world at the expense of the British and the French Empires. And who is such a fool as to think it will voluntarily return these bases at the end of the war? American troops are now to be found all over the British Empire, including England and Northern Ireland and also India. Everywhere within the Empire, American troops are under their own command and in some places, as in Australia and New Zealand, even British troops are under American command. In other words, America is slowly but surely carrying out a peaceful military occupation of the British Empire.

As the military occupation is proceeding, the Americans are gradually asserting themselves in the political sphere as well. A shining example of this American self-assertion is the fact that American troops in

England and in other parts of the Empire are above the law of the land. They are directly under Washington and under the jurisdiction of American Law; consequently, the Americans today have the same extra-territorial rights which the British enjoyed for a long time in China, Egypt and other countries.

A recent example of American self-assertion at the cost of Britain is the manner in which General de Gaulle and his claims were brushed aside and Admiral Darlan, the protégé of the White House, was pitchforked into General de Gaulle's place in North Africa, in spite of all protests from the junior partner in the Anglo-American alliance. I confess that I was staggered the other day when the B.B.C. announced that Prime Minister Churchill had declared that the orders of an American, General Eisenhower, would be obeyed by the British authorities. One can hardly believe that the British Lion has been metamorphosed into a tame lamb by the master of the White House. But facts stare us in the face. The once almighty British Parliament cannot even venture to discuss in a public session the Darlan episode lest the American President be offended by it.

So far as India is concerned, my countrymen are aware that American troops, American technical missions, American diplomatic agents are already there. The Americans are now openly saying that the Americans in India are not under the jurisdiction of London but of Washington, and along with this announcement, the White House is taking steps to tighten American hold over India at the expense of the British Government. No doubt Churchill and Amery and their colleagues are submitting to every humiliation at the hands of the White House because they hope that they will thereby save the Empire somehow. But the American President is a superior tactician. While thankfully accepting the abject submission and surrender of British politicians, he is relentlessly proceeding with his own plan of taking over the British Empire, lock, stock and barrel. He has now sent out as Ambassador to India Mr William Phillips, because he was not content with the regime of the British Viceroy, Lord Linlithgow. India will now have a new master in place of the worn-out Scotch Marquis. For the present, Mr Phillips will be content with being the power behind the throne. But if the American plan were to prevail and the United States were somehow to win the war, then Mr Phillips would openly step into the shoes of the last British Viceroy. But India has no desire to substitute an American Pro-Consul for a British Viceroy, and we must, therefore, fight this latest American threat to India.

Countrymen and friends, let us have no illusions about the role of the United States in the politics of the British Empire and of India. We thankfully recognise the fact that a large section of the American people have sympathy for Indian independence, but unfortunately they are powerless to influence their own Government. So far as American official *policy towards India is concerned, it is as imperialistic as that of Britain*. If the White House really wanted to do so, it could have forced Whitehall to concede independence to India, but instead of doing that, it is itself carrying out a peaceful occupation of India and now Mr Phillips is going out to India to make the necessary social contacts with the Indian people, so that in the fullness of time he and the U.S. Army can quietly replace Lord Linlithgow and the British Army and take over the reins of Government. Countrymen, beware of him. Boycott him.

Anglo-American propagandists have been conducting a terrific propaganda campaign regarding what would happen to this poor world if the Tripartite Powers win this war, and they are shedding crocodile tears over the fate of the small nations and of the minorities. But we the people of India, who represent one-fifth of the human race, know what will be our fate if the so-called United Nations were to win this war by any chance. The Atlantic Charter, of which we have heard so much, is as much a scrap of paper as President Wilson's Fourteen Points in the last war. But the application of even this scrap of paper has been officially denied to India because the Anglo-American Powers stand for an imperialist policy in India in an open and unashamed manner.

British plans for post-war India have been made, and if British politicians were to have their own way, they would split up India into four or five States under a strong imperialist Government which would exploit the country more intensively than hitherto, in order to make up for their losses in this war. The Union Jack would then fly not only over the capital of India as at present, but over the capitals of 'Hindustan', 'Pakistan', 'Rajasthan', 'Khalistan' and 'Pathanistan'. And the Indian people would be given a British guarantee of permanent enslavement. Let Mr M.A. Jinnah and his Muslim League ponder over this.

Let us now consider what would happen to India if the British Empire were to be sent into compulsory liquidation by the White House and Wall Street, and if the American President became the 'Director of the World'. We are having a foretaste of this in the policy and the behaviour of the American Government today. This Government has always demanded an open-door policy in China; but do the people of China or Japan or India or of any Asiatic countries have an open door in the United States of America? Why has immigration to the U.S.A. been denied to the nations of Asia? Why have a large number of Indians, who had long been settled in the States, been denied citizenship rights in that country? If the Atlantic Charter has any meaning or significance for humanity, should not this insult and humiliation to India be removed at once? And if the ruling classes of America shed crocodile tears over the fate of the minorities elsewhere, why do they not first put their own house in order? Why do they not put a stop to the lynching of negroes, which goes on even today? Why do they not remove the poll tax and similar disabilities imposed on the American negroes? And if they profess to stand for freedom, democracy and fair play, why do they not remove the social disabilities from which the negroes have to suffer in the States.

No, my countrymen, all this talk and all these high-sounding professions of American politicians and their President are sanctimonious hypocrisies, just plain tommy rot. And if Mr William Phillips were to replace the Marquis of Linlithgow and if the Yankee troops were to replace the Gordon Highlanders, India would remain where she is today. India's only hope of salvation lies in a complete overthrow of Anglo-American imperialism.

Countrymen and friends, it is my duty to inform you that our enemies are now trying to play once again the trump-card which they used during the last war. That trump-card was atrocity propaganda against the then enemies of British imperialism. But the world has not forgotten entirely the lies and the blood-curdling stories spread by British propagandists at that time. Who has not read such books as 'Figures' or 'Crewe House' and 'Wartime Falsehoods' written by eminent British publicists on the subject of British propaganda during that war? Who does not still remember the confessions made by General Charteris and others after the war about the lies that they had deliberately and diabolically spread against their enemies while the war was on? The world is wiser today as a result of that experience, and moreover, the development of the radio has now made it possible to expose the falsity of British propaganda at every step. So far as India is concerned I know that all this atrocity propaganda will fall flat. The Indian people know, perhaps better than anybody else, what British domination means. The foundation of British rule in India was laid by Robert Clive whom history has convincingly proved to have been a forgerer. The British Empire in India was built on bribery, treachery and fraud and not as a result of military prowess. During the long struggle for power in India, there is no cruelty, there is no atrocity that the British have not committed in that country. Who does not know that in our revolution of 1857 innocent men were bound hand and foot and shot dead by cannon fire. From 1857 till today, during a period of peace, the British police and military have indulged in every form of terror and brutality in order to break the backbone of the people. The official report of the British Government on the Jallianwalla Bagh massacre in 1919 accuses the British authorities and the British Army of inhuman cruelty, unwarranted massacre, and of every form of humiliation and torture including dishonouring of helpless women. And even after 1919, the lives of Indian men and the honour of Indian women have always been regarded by the British police and the military as mere playthings. Who in India does not know of the sufferings of the people of Midnapore in Bengal in 1930, when homes and villages were burnt and their womenfolk dishonoured because they were conducting a peaceful campaign for non-payment of taxes? The atrocities in the prisoners' camp at Hubli and in towns of Dacca and Chittagong in 1931 are known to every household in Bengal. After the beginning of this war, I have seen with my own eyes the photos of beheaded Burmese sent by British tommies in Burma to their families in Britain. Such sadism is possible only among British tommies, and to cap everything, is there any parallel to be found for the atrocities now being perpetrated on unarmed men, women and children by the British police and military in India for their crime in demanding freedom? It does not lie in the mouths of Britishers to accuse anybody of committing atrocities when they are themselves past-masters in that game.

Apart from the fact that India's only hope of emancipation lies in the defeat of Anglo-American imperialism, we have to acknowledge quite objectively that this war will end with the complete dismemberment of the British Empire. Part of this Empire will probably gravitate towards the United States of America. Large parts of it will emancipate themselves once for all and some parts of it will probably be distributed among the other Powers. Mr Winston Churchill may not like to preside over the liquidation of the Empire and undoubtedly he is thoroughly sincere when he says so, but the policy that he has been following will inevitably lead the Empire to its doom. His presence at the helm of affairs in Whitehall is the surest guarantee for us that there will be no compromise between India and Britain on the road to liberty. I therefore pray that in the interests of India and in the larger interests of humanity he may be left to rule over the destinies of the British Empire till the hour of its final dissolution strikes.

It is not because of any wishful thinking that I am convinced that Britain will be defeated and India will emerge independent out of this war. There is a common world strategy against the Anglo-American Powers in this war, which did not exist in the last. Thanks to the Berlin–Rome–Tokyo Axis, Britain has nowhere any peace now, neither in the Atlantic, nor in the Mediterranean, nor in the Pacific. The age of sea power is over, and in spite of all her naval supremacy, Britain now finds that the weapon of blockade, which brought about the final decision in the last war is now working against her. Consequently, the food situation is just as serious in Britain today as it is on the European continent. The problem will become much more than serious in future. The art of warfare has been so revolutionised that the old imperialist Powers are now at a disadvantage. Time which in the last war was for Britain and her Allies, is now working against them; and last but not the least, the Anglo-American Powers have sustained a crushing defeat in Europe and in Asia, where the fate of the war has been conclusively decided. The Anglo-American Powers and their propagandists know very well how desperate their position is; and in order to divert the attention of the world from these dark facts they have staged a campaign in North-West Africa at the expense of the helpless and defeated French Empire. The object of this campaign is more propagandist than military; and simultaneously with the opening of this campaign, the output of propaganda has been purposely intensified. At one time the B.B.C. used to say that United States of America would save the British Empire, then it went on to say that Soviet Russia, with the help of General

Winter, would save the position. But when the Axis proved the falsity of this, the B.B.C. has now come out with the assertion that the battle of Africa will turn the tide of the war. From these facts you have to come to the irresistible conclusion that the Anglo-Americans, despite all their propaganda bombast and lying face inevitable and shattering defeat. They are doomed, and steadily they are moving towards total defeat.

In the circumstances, we Indians should mobilise all our resources and put in all that we have in a last struggle against British imperialism. The British who have exploited India for more than 150 years, are now on their last legs; and in this dark hour of the British Empire is India's opportunity. If we can strike hard and with determination, I have every confidence that we shall be able to destroy British power in India and attain our freedom. This can be our last fight for freedom. And I hope and trust that when the history of this last fight is written it will be possible to say that the Indians all over the world fought in this battle.

In conclusion, I would like to warn my countrymen in Bengal that difficult days are in store for them, much blood will flow in that eastern province, but our countrymen there should not fear it. It is Bengal that opened the door to the British in India, and Bengal should now show them the way out.

In the past, the British used India as a base and also used India's resources for attacking and conquering Burma. Now that the British have been expelled from Burma, they want once again to use India, and particularly Bengal, for trying to reconquer that land. They are thereby deliberately dragging war to the soil of India. Bengal will accordingly have the experience of the horrors of total war before any other province. But, let Bengal be proud of it. The task of the vanguard is always a difficult one, but it is also a glorious one. I am confident that Bengal will rise to the occasion and fulfil her historic role.

Once again the Sun of Freedom will rise in the East.
Inquilab Zindabad. Azad Hind Zindabad!

33

Somewhere Near India

LETTER TO GERMAN FOREIGN MINISTER
VON RIBBENTROP, 5 DECEMBER 1942

Your Excellency,

I wanted to address Your Excellency immediately after my return from Rome, but I have been delayed owing to physical indisposition. Before, I proceed to speak about my own plans and desires I wish to say something about the situation in India.

I am glad to be able to report that in spite of the recent developments in Africa and in Western Europe, the situation in India has not, from our point of view, worsened in any way. Rather, the general mood is now more anti-British than before. The following factors account for the present situation in India.

(1) North Africa is too far from India—and military developments there do not have much effect on India.

(2) Field Marshall Rommel's present withdrawal still makes people hope that he will be in a position to take the offensive in Libya again in future.

(3) Military, the most impressive and the most important thing for India is the success of the Japanese armed forces. So long as the Japanese Army stands on the frontier of India, any local, temporary set backs which any of the Tripartite Powers may suffer in another theatre of war, cannot have any marked effect on India.

(4) The utterances of the British Prime Minister and of other British politicians in recent weeks have further embittered the feelings of the Indian people.

(5) The removal of Sir Stafford Cripps from the War Cabinet and from the leadership of the House of Commons indicated more

clearly to India that the policy of the British Government in future is going to be a rank imperialistic one.

(6) Last but not least, while present propaganda from London may have some influence in certain parts of Europe, it can have no influence on the Indian people. So much distrust in British propaganda has been engendered by us in India that we can rest assured that as long as the Indian leaders are in prison and British policy continues to be an imperialistic one, propaganda from London will fall on deaf ears.

The task of our own propaganda now is to further strengthen Indian distrust in all propaganda coming from Anglo-American sources. At the same time, we have to tell our countrymen that in case the position of the Anglo-Americans were to improve locally for a time in any part of the world—we have only to tighten our belts and work and fight even harder than before. The idea of a common struggle against a common enemy based on a common strategy has to be stressed more and more in future.

Viewed from the standpoint of a common world-strategy, it would appear that the importance of India in the common struggle against the Anglo-American powers has increased considerably. My presence in the Far East at this juncture has, in consequence, become more imperatively necessary than before. *I could do much more for my country, if I could be somewhere near India.* I could then help India to play a role in this war which would be of importance not only to India herself, but also to the common struggle against the common foe. India is a place where one could strike directly at England and, indirectly, at America. It is naturally a disappointment for me that at the eleventh hour my journey to the Far East had to be abandoned, owing to reasons that were purely technical, though everything possible had been done from the side of the German Government to help in the matter. Nevertheless, I remain an optimist and I have an intuitive feeling that a way will be found to make the journey possible.

I believe that it is technically possible for the German Government to help me to travel to the Far East—either by aeroplane or by submarine or by ship. There is a certain amount of risk undoubtedly in this undertaking, but so is there in every undertaking. That risk I shall gladly and voluntarily take. At the same time, I believe in my destiny and I therefore believe that this endeavour will succeed. I would be profoundly grateful to Your Excellency and to the German Government for the necessary help in this matter—regardless of the difficulty or risk or inconvenience entailed thereby. And the sooner I could travel, the better it would be for India and for the common cause.

Assuring Your Excellency of my warmest esteem,
I am,

Yours respectfully,
SUBHAS CHANDRA BOSE

34

The Situation in Europe

BROADCAST, 7 DECEMBER 1942[1]

After speaking to you last from the Short Wave Station in Berlin, in October, about two months ago, it was my intention to leave Europe and return to my Headquarters, from where I could address you again over the Azad Hind Radio. But unfortunately I fell ill with influenza which kept me confined to my room for a few weeks. And, thereafter, I decided to make a short tour of Europe once again, in order to gather first-hand impressions of recent developments. During this tour, I have been in parts of Europe which are called 'Occupied' territories. I have been in some of the new States like Slovakia that have come into existence after the outbreak of the present war, and I have been to countries like Italy, which are actively engaged in a grim struggle with Anglo-American imperialism. I am, therefore, in a position to form a correct and absolutely unbiased picture of the situation in this continent. While making this study tour, I have of course been able to study the war situation in general and the Indian situation in particular. Finding myself in Berlin once again I am now accepting the hospitality of the short-wave radio station here in order to speak to you on the situation as I see it, and on our tasks at home.

It is not necessary for me to make a propaganda speech. Nor is it necessary for me to indulge in rambling utterances as men in the street are in the habit of doing. I shall speak to you as before, in a plain and matter of fact manner. People who are inclined to be impatient will naturally be disappointed that things have not moved fast enough during the last two months, and they may think that the situation remains

---

[1] Broadcast from Berlin on 7 December 1942, and reprinted in *Azad Hind* (11/12, 1942).

fundamentally the same as it was in September and October last. I must tell you frankly, however, that I do not share this view. The war has reached a stage when time is working definitely for the Tripartite Powers and their Allies, and against our common enemy. Unlike the last war we find that in this war the economic blockade is working against Britain and not against Germany. Moreover, the British Empire has been steadily losing one part of its territories to its adversaries and another part to its great ally. Consequently, the longer the war lasts the more shall we see with our own eyes the rapid disintegration and the ultimate liquidation of the once vast and powerful British Empire. Despite all the efforts of the high priest of imperialism, Mr Winston Churchill, the British Empire is going the way of all other empires of the past and the only problem that remains to be solved is as to who will be the heirs and successors of this Empire.

We have learnt from world history that it is an irony of fate that the staunchest champions of imperialism always manage to hasten its end. Similarly, we have seen in India that reactionary and oppressive rulers like Lord Curzon always do more to rouse and strengthen the forces of nationalism than the so-called 'friends of India' like Lord Ripon or Lord Irwin. We should indeed be grateful to Providence that at the most opportune moment he ordained that Mr Winston Churchill should be at the helm of affairs in Britain. Mr Churchill's premiership is for India the surest guarantee that there will be no compromise between the British Government and the Indian nationalists and that India will achieve her goal of independence before long. Let us, therefore, pray that he may continue to rule over the destinies of the British Empire during the hour of its final and gruesome collapse.

Meanwhile, let Liberals and Democrats like Sir Stafford Cripps who in reality constitute a greater menace to India's independence, be thrown out because such Liberals and Democrats can only create confusion in the minds of Indian nationalists. Let imperialism based on tanks and machine guns rule in India so that the Indian people may see for themselves what British imperialism really is, and in that knowledge refuse to have anything to do with Britain.

However one might judge military events during the last two or three months, there can be no doubt that for India the political situation has, during this period, become more favourable. Mr Churchill and his colleagues have through their utterances and their behaviour, clarified the situation once and for all. Every Indian can now understand clearly what Britain's war aims are; what the Atlantic Charter and the 'New Order' of the so-called United Nations signify to the poor Indian people. Every Indian is, therefore, convinced more than ever before, that for him there is but one road to freedom and that is the destruction of the gigantic British Empire. If the enemies of British imperialism help India to achieve that objective, all the better for India, for her tasks will then be so much easier. But if not, the Indian people must gird up their loins and solemnly resolve to effect their own salvation through their own efforts, sufferings and sacrifices. Between British Imperialism and Indian Nationalism no compromise is possible. One must perish for the other to live and since Indian Nationlism shall live, British Imperialism must die.

Friends, we see that while in Britain rank imperialists have taken charge of public affairs and are managing things in their own way, in the United States of America two voices can be heard. Large sections of the public are genuinely interested in Indian independence and openly criticise the American imperialists. On the other hand the Government and those who hold the reins of power are pursuing a policy which can only be described as 'American Imperialism.' In fact, a definite school of thought has grown up in the United States of America, which loudly proclaims that the world belongs to the United States of America, and this theory of an American world-empire has already found an echo across the Atlantic, and several prominent and serious British thinkers are directly or indirectly giving their support to it. They are, however, of the opinion that, while the British should recognise and accept American supremacy in world affairs, America for her part should allow the British Empire to exist with all its dependencies and not interfere in the internal affairs of that Empire.

The partnership of President Roosevelt and Premier Churchill is going to endure, and the President knows that Churchill, his junior partner, will go on taking orders from him so long as the future of the British Empire and its continuance depends on American assistance. The Indians should have found out by now that in actual practice they can expect no help from the so-called United Nations in their struggle for liberty, and the latest developments in Anglo-American relations more than confirm the correctness of this view. The Indian people have therefore to fight their own battle and any help from outside, should it be necessary, can only be forthcoming from the enemies of the so-called United Nations.

In this connection I should like to inform my countrymen all over the world that while Mr Churchill and important circles in Britain are busy preparing plans for post-war reconstruction there is no place for the free India in their scheme of things. They hope to solve the Indian problem, not by applying the principles of the Atlantic Charter to India, but by adopting radical and drastic measures in order to crush Indian nationalism, so that in the post-war world there may be a number of States in the territories that have from time immemorial been known as India, and that all States will be equally under the heel of the British. I know that some of my countrymen formerly held the view that the British Government, in view of its precarious position, would recognise the freedom of India, and thereby try to secure a useful ally in its fight with the Tripartite Powers. But I think that British strategy will now be clear to even a child of ten. The British Government, thanks to Mr Winston Churchill and to the ruling classes in Britain, will not surrender to the Indian people. Whatever surrender has to be made it will be made only to the White House. And the sacrifice that Britain will have to make to the United States will be compensated by the plight of India, which will be much worse in future. In other words, while John Bull is bled white in order to satisfy Uncle Sam, India is to bleed white in order to keep John Bull alive. Consequently, so long as the British Empire exists the future of India can only mean the most painful enslavement.

It should by now be apparent to my countrymen that the so-called United Nations are trying to develop something like the common world strategy. But this is a poor imitation of the common world strategy of the Tripartite Powers, of the Berlin–Rome–Tokyo axis. In accordance with the idea of a common world strategy, of which the Anglo-Americans have talked so much, the Anglo-American powers, in particular Britain, have been planning for a 'Second Front' which is to be set up in Europe as soon as possible. Unwillingly and under extreme pressure the Anglo-Americans made the experiment at several places in Europe, but in every case they met with familiar failure.

At the last resort, in order to make some show of a 'Second Front', they made an attack on African territory, which neither belonged to nor was occupied by any of the Tripartite Powers, but which belonged to the French Empire and was purposely left in the hands of the French as a friendly gesture to a defeated enemy. This sudden attack on a helpless nation and undefended territory, preceded by intrigues with some of the local authorities, is now being trumpeted from London and New York as a great military feat. Neutral spectators judge this military feat on a par with the occupation of Madagascar and Reunion Island, which also belonged to the French Empire. It is meant to hide the defeats of Britain in other theatres of war, which are of real significance to the final result of the present struggle. It is meant to divert attention from the real issues and as a sop to the Soviet Government which has been making insistent demands for a 'Second Front' in Europe.

Friends, let us now dispassionately sum up the situation as one sees it today. The Anglo-American powers have been driven out from the Far East and their own fleet now lies buried in the watery grave of the Pacific. From Europe, British power has been annihilated completely, and all talks of a 'Second Front' are childish dreams. All that the Anglo-American powers can now do is to seek battles and wars on the African continent at the expense of the helpless French Empire. But it is Europe and Asia, and not Africa that will decide the fate of this war. And so far as Europe and Asia are concerned, the prospect for the Anglo-American powers and their Allies is as black as can be. The British authorities have raised a hue and cry by radio speeches over the landing of American troops on undefended French territory in North Africa. I wonder what sort of propaganda they would have indulged in if they had really won a battle against a superior adversary. The tactics of British propaganda prove very clearly that public morale in Britain has sunk so low that artificial stimulants in the form of such British propaganda are necessary in order to keep up the spirit of the British people. For a time the B.B.C. was telling the world that the U.S.A. would save Britain from defeat. Then it adopted the argument that Soviet Russia would save Britain from disaster. Now it is saying that Africa would help to turn the tide of war. Never for one single occasion have I heard a Britisher say during the last three years what a great British Prime Minister once declared in another historical speech, 'England will save herself by her own exertions.'

No friends, those days are gone for the British Empire and are gone forever, and we now see with our own eyes the rapid collapse of what was once a vast and powerful Empire. I may tell you quite frankly that reviewing the war situation as a whole, in the light of the latest events, I feel more optimistic than ever before. Nothing can stand between the Indian people and their goal of complete independence. We must however participate more actively and more vigorously in the common struggle, having a common goal. There is one common world strategy for the maintenance and perpetuation of the old order with all the injustice on which it was based, and the answer to it is a common world strategy for the destruction of the old order and the creation of a new one.

Coming now to the situation in India I want, first, to congratulate you once again upon your achievements during the last few months. It came as a pleasant surprise to the world where owing to prolonged British propaganda, it was not expected that the unarmed Indian people would be able to put up such a brave fight against such a powerful enemy, armed with tanks, machine-guns and aeroplanes. The British authorities have been trying continuously to conceal the real facts of the Indian situation from the outside world, but in spite of all such sinister efforts the whole world has been informed regularly of what has been happening in India and what is agreeable for the Indian people is that, even in the camp of the so-called United Nations, there is a great deal of sympathy and support for India's demand for independence.

Friends, I have already stressed that we are now engaged in a common struggle against a common foe. In this struggle India and the countries of the Near East have to play a more active part in future. It is for you, who have been enslaved, that the British Empire has to be overthrown and your responsibility is therefore truly great. And the responsibility of the Indian people is the greatest of all. India is the corner stone of the British Empire. In fact it is India that has made the Empire and it is now the task of India to crush that Empire and to help in the liberation of humanity.

There is no doubt that during the course of the national struggle the Indian people have suffered much. But they must be prepared to suffer even more. The path of liberty is never strewn with roses. Suffering is still in store for our people. More blood, innocent blood, will yet flow over the sacred soil of Hindustan before we can expect to be liberated. But the blood of martyrs is always the price of freedom and hence we are prepared to pay that price. Our victory is assured beyond the shadow of doubt. Remember the slogan that I recommended to you the other day, 'Two years and one hundred thousand lives'! We must be prepared to voluntarily sacrifice one hundred thousand lives in the course of the struggle. If we do so freedom will be ours once and for all.

Friends, some of my British listeners sitting in the offices of the B.B.C. have been upset that I have not yet redeemed my promise to return home and participate in the final phase of our struggle. I would like to advise them to have some patience. Meanwhile, I may assure them that my pledge, given not to the British Government but to my own people, will be redeemed in the fullness of time. As sure as day follows night, the present world war will bring about a complete dismemberment of the British Empire. As sure as day follows night, India will emerge from the struggle as an independent state. And as sure as day follows night, I will live to participate in the final struggle for our liberty, not from abroad, but at home side by side with the comrades who have been bravely carrying on the fight, while I have been away on duty.

Inquilab Zindabad. Azad Hind Zindabad.

35

The Duty of Patriotic Indians

BROADCAST, 1 JANUARY 1943[1]

It is lucky that military developments during the last year have facilitated our struggle for freedom. Allied attempts to open their much talked of 'Second Front' in Europe have failed miserably. The Axis forces have the upper hand in North Africa. The gallant Japanese have delivered fatal blows to the Anglo-Americans in the Far East and the British Empire is fast disintegrating. The Japanese maintain their superiority in the S.W. Pacific and on the Indian front. In short, British and American influence has completely been eliminated from the East as well as the West. The war has now entered its final phase. The Axis Powers are invincible and time is working in their favour.

In the last world war the Allies had command over the major part of the Continent, but today, they have been ousted from Europe. France was the main theatre of the last war, while she is out of the game today. Russia was then on the offensive. She is now on the defensive. German forces have penetrated into the very heart of the Soviet Union. Both Britain and America had complete mastery of the seas during the last war, whereas today, their combined land, air and naval forces are no match for those of the Axis. The last war was confined to Europe and the Middle East, while the flames of the present have spread almost all over the world, thanks to Axis domination of the air, land and sea. The Mediterranean was under British control during the last war, but today, the condition of Britain there is very precarious. The Allies blockaded Germany during the last war, now it is the other way about. Germany has blockaded Britain.

---

[1] Broadcast over Berlin Radio on 1 January 1943.

THE DUTY OF PATRIOTIC INDIANS

The Axis Powers have unlimited resources, manpower and vast stores of food grains at their disposal. The condition of the Allies is going from bad to worse every day, and shortage of shipping has become a serious problem for Allied statesmen. The active participation of Japan in this war guarantees Axis victory. Britain had long been busy fortifying the N.W.F.P. She began fortifying Eastern India in 1941. Singapore, which the British had been fortifying for the last 20 years, was occupied by the Japanese in seven days. Taking all these facts into consideration, we can safely say that the British are doomed.

Indians should now come into the field and play their part in the crusade against the Anglo-Americans. They should shake off the British yoke. After the defeat of the British, Indians will have their own independent Government.

Indians and Indian nationals abroad! I know that you have full confidence in me. The consequences of this war are plain, the British Empire will inevitably disappear and India will be a free country. Indians should, therefore, extend their wholehearted co-operation to the Axis Powers and fight side by side with them. Those who refuse to take part in the Indian war of independence are traitors. Indian nationals in foreign countries have also a role in the present struggle. We should carry on our struggle in spite of British tyranny and oppression. Jails and shootings should not dishearten us. Every Indian should be determined to face hardships. Sacrifice and action will help you to attain your long-cherished goal–Freedom.

36

Independence Day

SPEECH, 26 JANUARY 1943[1]

Ladies and Gentlemen!

On this day, 26 January, Indians in every part of the world assemble to observe their Independence Day. On this day they gather together under their national flag for the purpose of reaffirming their underlying faith in independence, and their unshakable determination to carry on the national struggle till victory is achieved. On this day in India, the tri-colour flag is hoisted in every home, processions are taken out everywhere and meetings and demonstrations are held all over the country, where the 'Independence Manifesto is' read and solemnly

---

[1] Broadcast from Berlin on 26 January 1943 and printed in *Azad Hind* (1/2, 1943). This speech was originally delivered in German; but immediately afterwards Netaji broadcast this speech in English. Berlin Radio relayed the celebrations from Berlin and the commentator first read out the Independence Day pledge of the Indian National Congress and then described the scene. He said: 'We are present at a big meeting in Berlin on the occasion of the Independence Day of India. Many hundreds of guests have assembled to hear an address by Subhas Chandra Bose. There are a great many Indians here, and representatives of many other nations of Europe, all invited by the Central Committee of Independent India. There are many Germans, Italians, Japanese and many high officials of the Foreign Office, officers of the Wehrmacht and members of the National Socialist Party. Among the guests are the Grand Mufti of Jerusalem and the Prime Minister of Iraq, Rashid Ali el Gilani—a very colourful and eminent gathering. The Hall is decorated with beautiful flower arrangements—red tulips and white lilacs. Now Subhas Chandra Bose—the great leader of Independent India, gets up and walks towards the speaker's chair. He is dressed in black sherwani. There is a thunderous applause and cheering as he comes up. Subhas Bose is speaking in German. Of course, many of you will not understand, so we have made arrangements to let you hear his address in English. Subhas Chandra Bose has kindly agreed to speak to you in English. Now here is Subhas Bose speaking to you.' Then followed the speech which has been printed here.

adopted. Not always are the Indian people allowed to perform this national ceremony without let or hindrance. Again and again they are obliged to act in defiance of police prohibition and in direct opposition to the armed forces of the British Crown. Thus in 1931, just 12 years ago, while leading a peaceful procession on Independence Day as Mayor of India's largest city, Calcutta, I and my fellow processionists were attacked and brutally assaulted by British mounted police till permanent marks of injury were left on our persons. But our lot was nevertheless better than that of those who had to face the bayonet and rifle-shot.

Ladies and Gentlemen! Thanks to the hospitality of the German Government, my compatriots and I are able to observe Independence Day this year in Germany, in a solemn and peaceful manner. But our thoughts naturally go out to our people at home, who have to observe Independence Day in defiance of tear gas and police batons, bayonets and machine guns. So wonderful is the Atlantic Charter, for which the Allied powers are fighting, that in India all public meetings and demonstrations have been permanently prohibited, and a reign of terror has been let loose over the whole land, simply because the Indian National Congress had the audacity to demand freedom and democracy for the Indian people.

Experience during the last thirty years has opened the eyes of the whole world to the importance of propaganda in modern life and especially in modern warfare. It will be generally admitted that Britain was the first to use the weapon of modern propaganda against her enemies on a large scale and she did it to great effect. Among those who have suffered as a result of this false, sinister—and sometimes subtle—propaganda—stands India. Very late in this day have we Indians realised that in fighting one's enemies, it is necessary not only to have a just cause, but also to convince the world that one's cause is just. Whenever I have been outside India, I have been staggered to find how effective British propaganda against India has been throughout the world. The most painful experience for me has been to hear from the mouths of friends, the self-same arguments that die-hard, anti-Indian British propagandists are in the habit of trotting out.

To offer some kind of moral justification for British domination and exploitation of India, British propagandists have depicted it as a land where there is no unity, where the people are eternally fighting among themselves, and where the strong hand of Britain is necessary to maintain order and ensure progress. But these presumptuous Britishers conveniently forget that long before their forefathers knew anything about administration or national unity—in fact, long before the Romans came to Britain to teach culture and civilisation to the uncivilised Britons—India had not only an advanced culture and civilisation but a modern Empire founded by Chandragupta extending from Cape Comorin in the South to Afghanistan in the north—an empire that was geographically larger than the India of today. And India is a country where the past has not been forgotten as in Babylon, Egypt or Greece, but where history and tradition live in our blood and in the marrow of our bones. It is because of this national self-consciousness that neither political domination nor economic impoverishment has been able to kill our soul. We measure history not in decades—not in centuries—but in thousands of years. Consequently, when misfortune and ill luck overtake us, we do not lose our nerve. We know that if we persevere and fight on—we shall once again come to the top of the wave.

To us, life is one long unending wave. It is God manifesting himself in the infinite variety of creation. It is 'Leela'—an eternal play of forces. In this cosmic interplay of forces—there is not only sunshine, but there is also darkness. There is not only joy, but there is also sorrow. There is not only a rise, but there is also a fall. If we do not lose faith in ourselves and in our divinity—we shall move on through darkness, sorrow and degradation towards renewed sunshine, joy and progress.

Ladies and Gentleman! I apologise to you for digressing into the domain of philosophy. But if you want to understand India, you will have to understand the soul of India—the eternal faith which keeps us alive and youthful till today—the inner strength which makes us look forward to a new chapter in our history of freedom, progress and prosperity. It is difficult to understand such things in a land where Locke and Hume, Mill and Spencer represent the greatest philosophers. But in the land of Kant and Hegel, Goethe and Schopenhauer, Schlegel and Ruckert, Max Müller and Deussen—India is understood and will be understood.

The clash between India and England—political, economic and cultural—gave us a rude awakening and helped to knock out the temporary slumber, which had overtaken the Indian people in the eighteenth and nineteenth centuries. There has, however, been one experience in all our contact with Britain, which has been particularly painful to us. In the scale of values, which the British people cherish—morality, art and culture do not have their proper place. What is admired and respected by them above everything is the capacity to fight and to kill. What is also important is that in the occupation of India, the British used not only arms but also the weapons of bribery, treachery and every form of corruption. When the British first occupied a part of India, namely the province of Bengal, they came into touch with a people who were highly developed in art and philosophy but these people were nevertheless looked down upon, because the British regarded them to be no good as fighters. When the people realised after some time that what carries weight with the British is force and not art or morality—they began to use the bomb and the revolver. Since then, they have been respected by the Britisher—though feared and intensely hated. And the whole of India today knows that the only logic which Britain understands and respects is the logic of force.

Perhaps, a somewhat similar experience has been undergone by Japan, though under quite different circumstances. So long as Japan lived in dignified isolation and devoted her whole energy to her internal development—cultural, artistic and economic—she did not draw the admiration or the attention of the outside world. But when she demonstrated in 1905 that she could beat Imperial Russia in modern warfare—she immediately rose in the estimation of the whole world. This experience of Japan has been a lesson not only for India but for the other enslaved nations of Asia as well.

The greatest folly and mistake of our predecessors was their inability to realise at the very beginning, the real character and role of the Britishers who came to India. They had probably thought that like the innumerable tribes that had wandered to India in the past and had made India their home, the British were just another such tribe. It was much later that they realised that the British had come to conquer and plunder and not to settle down in India. As soon as this was generally understood all over the country, a mighty revolution broke out in 1857, which has been incorrectly called by English historians 'the Sepoy Mutiny' but which is regarded by the Indian people as the First War of Independence. In the Great Revolution of 1857, the British were on the point of being thrown out of the country but partly through superior strategy and partly through luck—they won at the end. Then there followed a reign of terror, the parallel of which it is difficult to find in history. Wholesale massacres took place in the course of which innocent men were bound hand and foot and were blown up from the mouth of cannon.

Organised British rule in India dates from the year 1858—that is, after the failure of the great revolution of 1857. If prior to this period India could live and prosper for thousands of years without the help of Britain, she can do the same in future, when she is free once again.

After the revolution of 1857, the British realised that they could not hold India for long by sheer brute force. They therefore, proceeded to disarm the country. And the second greatest folly and mistake that our predecessors committed was to submit to disarmament. If they had not given up their arms so easily, probably the history of India since 1857 would have been different from what it has been. Having once disarmed the country completely, it has been possible for the British to hold India with the help of a small but efficient modern army.

Along with disarmament, the newly established British Government, now controlled directly from London, commenced its policy of 'divide and rule'. This policy of 'divide and rule' has been the fundamental basis of British rule from 1858 till today. For nearly 40 years the policy was to keep India divided by keeping three-fourths of the people directly under British control and the remaining one-fourth under the Indian Princes. Simultaneously, the British Government showed a great deal of partiality for the big landlords in British India. By the beginning of the present century, the British realised, however, that they could no longer dominate India by simply playing the Princes and the big landlords against the people. Then they discovered the Muslim problem in the year 1906, when Lord Minto was Viceroy. Prior to this there was no such problem in India. In the great revolution of 1857, Hindus and Muslims had fought side by side against the British and it was under the flag of Bahadur Shah, a Muslim, that India's first war of Independence had been fought.

During the last World War, when the British found that further political concessions would have to be made to the Indian people, they realised that it was not enough to try and divide the Muslims from the rest of the population and they then set about trying to divide the Hindus themselves. In this way they discovered the caste problem in 1918, and suddenly became the champions and the liberators of the so-called 'Depressed Classes'. Till the year 1937, Britain had hoped to keep India divided by posing as champions of the Princes, the Muslims and the so-called 'Depressed Classes'. In the General Election held under the new Constitution of 1935, they found, however, to their great surprise that all their tricks and bluffs had failed and that strong nationalist feeling permeated the whole nation and every section of it. Consequently, British policy has now fallen back on its last hope. If the Indian people cannot be divided, then the country—India—has to be split up, geographically and politically. This is the plan called 'Pakistan' which emanated from the fertile brain of a Britisher and which has precedents in other parts of the British Empire. For instance, Ceylon, which belongs geographically and culturally to India, was separated from India long ago. Immediately after the last war, Ireland, which was always a unified state, was divided into Ulster and the Irish Free State. After the new constitution of 1935, Burma was separated from India. And if the present war had not intervened, Palestine would already have between divided into a Jewish State, an Arab State and a British corridor running between the two. Having themselves invented Pakistan—or the plan for dividing India—the British have been doing a colossal—but skilfull—propaganda in support of it.

Though the vast majority of the Indian Muslims want a free and independent India, though the President of the Indian National Congress today is Maulana Abul Kalam Azad, a Muslim, and though only a minority of the Indian Muslims support the idea of 'Pakistan', British propaganda throughout the world gives the impression that the Indian Muslims are not behind the national struggle for liberty and want India to be divided up. The British themselves know that what they propagated is quite false, but they nevertheless hope that by repeating a falsehood again and again, they will be able to make the world believe it.

And having themselves invented to divide India, they have so elaborated this plan that if they could manage things in their own way, they would divide India not into two states—as originally proposed—but into five or six states and all of these states would necessarily lie under the heel of Britain.

Ladies and Gentlemen! I have taken so much of your time in analysing British policy in India, because I want to tell you that though we have in British imperialism a cunning and diabolical enemy, we know our enemy inside out and there is no possibility of our being deceived again in future. When we have once sized up our enemy correctly, we shall be able to overthrow him. There is no possibility of a compromise between India and Britain. We have nothing in common and our national interests are diametrically opposed. The Tripartite Powers are today at war with British imperialism. British imperialism and Indian nationalism cannot exist simultaneously. The one must die if the other has to live and since Indian nationalism will live, British imperialism must die.

The struggle which is now going on in India is in reality a continuation of the great revolution of 1857. In the last four decades of the 19th Century, the Indian movement expressed itself in agitation in the Press and on the platform. This movement was crystallised into one organisation, when the Indian National Congress was inaugurated in 1885. The beginning of this century saw a new awakening in India and along with it new methods of struggle were devised. Thus, during the first two decades we see the economic boycott of British goods on the one side and revolutionary terrorism on the other. The Indian revolutionaries made a desperate attempt to overthrow British rule with the help of arms during the last war—at a time when Germany, Austria-Hungary and Turkey were fighting our enemy. But they, the Indian revolutionaries, were unfortunately crushed.

After the war India needed a new weapon of struggle, and at this psychological moment Mahatma Gandhi came forward with his method of Satyagraha or passive resistance. During the last 22 years, the Congress, under the Mahatma's leadership, has built up a powerful organisation all over the country, including the States of the Princes. It has awakened political life in the remotest village and among all sections of the people. Most important of all is the fact that the masses of India have learnt how to strike at a powerful enemy even without arms, and the Congress under Mahatmaji's leadership has demonstrated that it is possible to paralyse the administration with the weapons of passive resistance. In short, India has now a disciplined political organisation reaching the remotest villages with which a national struggle can be conducted and with the help of which—a new, independent state can be, later on, built up.

The younger generation in India has, however, learnt from the experience of the last 20 years that, while passive resistance can hold up or paralyse a foreign administration, it cannot overthrow or expel it without the use of physical force. Impelled by this experience, the people today are spontaneously passing on from passive resistance to active fighting, and that is why you read and hear today of the unarmed Indian people destroying railway, telegraph and telephone communications; setting fire to police stations, post offices and Government buildings, and using force in many other ways in order to overthrow the British yoke.

I have participated in all the campaigns from 1921 to 1941. During this period I have been in British custody eleven times and on most occasions without any trial in a court of law. From this experience, as well as from the information that I possess regarding the present campaign in India, I can assert without any exaggeration that it is impossible for the British Government to suppress the movement this time. There are internal and external causes which account for my optimism. Among internal causes I may say that the campaign is spread all over India, that the people of the Indian States are also participating in this all-India fight, and that the movement has spontaneously developed from passive resistance to active fighting. Among the external causes, I may say that India is not fighting alone this time. The Tripartite Powers and their Allies are also our allies in a common struggle, against a common foe and even the masses in India surely realise that India has now a glorious opportunity to achieve her liberty, which is indeed rare in history, and what is the most important of all is that there is a widespread conviction in India that this war will end only with the defeat and break-up of the British Empire.

We in India had always regretted that during the last war the then leaders had not utilised the war situation to our advantage. It was, therefore, necessary for me to leave India this time in order to establish direct personal contact with the enemies of British imperialism and thereby link up India's fight for freedom with the struggle of the Tripartite Powers against our old enemy, Britain. Though the Indian people must rely primarily on themselves for achieving their liberty, anything that weakens Britain automatically helps them and it would be indeed foolish of them not to take the fullest advantage of such assistance which fate and history has provided for them. Regarding my activities abroad, I may say that what I have been doing outside India has the fullest support of the vast majority of my countrymen. As a matter of fact, there is now full accord between Indians fighting at home and those working abroad for the common goal of India's emancipation.

I should not, however, give the impression that we are fully content with what has already been achieved at home. We are content only in so far as the movement is now a dynamic one and has developed into an active resistance and that it is too powerful to be crushed by the armed forces of the Anglo-American Powers. The present phase of the campaign has a two-fold object—to obstruct the administration of India and to destroy Britain's war production in that country. But, we must sooner or later pass on to the last phase of the struggle, namely, an armed revolution for destroying British Imperialism in India. How to achieve this task and how to bring the necessary help from outside in order to make that revolution a success is the problem that awaits solution.

It is my personal conviction that the present year, 1943, will be the year of decision and that during this year India must do the maximum that is possible for our common victory. The Allied Powers probably realise the significance of this year and that is why since New Year's Day they have been carrying on a terrific propaganda campaign. If one were to read or hear what London or New York now says, one would think that the Anglo-Americans have already won the war. But victories can no longer be won by bluffing and bumptious propaganda. The Anglo-Americans have also been conducting a blood-curdling atrocity propaganda against the Tripartite Powers, just as they did against Germany in the last war. But that, too, is too transparent to deceive anybody for a second time. That the Anglo-Americans should be forced to adopt such methods in order to bolster up their own morale shows clearly what their position really is. Anybody who takes a dispassionate and objective view of the entire war situation can come to only one conclusion, namely, that this war will end with victory of the Tripartite Powers.

This war offers not only India, but also all other enslaved nations of the British Empire a unique opportunity for throwing off the foreign yoke. It is a matter of gratification that the people in Iran and throughout the Arab world are also doing their utmost to utilise this opportunity for achieving their liberation. The fact that the leader of the Arab world—His Eminence the Grand Mufti and His Excellency the Prime Minister of Iraq, Raschid Ali El Gailani—now stand outside the clutches of British Imperialism is a source of joy and hope, not merely to the Arab world, but to the entire Orient.

Ladies and Gentlemen! We, the people of India, are convinced that we shall be freed before long, we have right to exist, not only for ourselves but for the sake of humanity, for India represents one-fifth of the human race. A free India will be able to contribute in a large measure to the culture and civilisation of the world. A free India will bring about the end of British Imperialism, which has been responsible for the enslavement, impoverishment and exploitation of large sections of the human race. A free India will mean the end of all those wars which have taken place in the past in Europe and elsewhere in the attempt to dominate India. A free India will mean that the countries of the Near, Middle and Far East will breathe freely, for there will be no power to threaten their freedom and security any longer. And, last but not least, a free India will be responsible for initiating a revolutionary change in the present economic order of the world.

I have no doubt that, with the single exception of Great Britain, a free India will be a blessing to the whole world and an advantage to every other nation desiring to have cultural and economic relations with her. The industrialisation of a vast country like India, inhabited by 388 millions of human beings, will have colossal and far-reaching repercussions throughout the modern industrial world. We who are engaged in the fight for India's liberation know exactly what we shall do in a free India. We are, therefore, preparing plans for national reconstruction for building up a new India. The task of reconstruction in free India is one which will interest not only the people of India but the entire civilised world as well.

Ladies and Gentlemen! In conclusion, I thank you from the bottom of my heart in the name of my country for the friendly sympathy you have demonstrated for our struggle, by participating in today's function. On our part, we assure you that we shall fight to the last, till our common enemy is overthrown and common victory is achieved. In this struggle—which is for India a life and death struggle—there will be but one end, our common victory.

Long Live the Tripartite Powers and their Allies!
Long Live Free India!

37

The Bluff and Bluster Corporation of British Imperialists

SPEECH, LATE JANUARY/EARLY FEBRUARY 1943[1]

Friends, when I took the unusual step of defying the British Government and departed from India, my principal objectives were two-fold. Firstly, to find out for myself the truth as to what is happening in the world, and secondly, to see if India has any allies in her fight for freedom. During the time that I have been away from home I have seen things with my own eyes and heard with my own ears. I have followed closely the propaganda war conducted by both sides in this world war. I am, therefore able to form an impartial and objective opinion as to what is really happening now and what is going to happen in the future. After this long, laborious and critical study of world affairs, there is not the slightest possibility of being misled or misguided in my judgment. I should also like to add that whatever I have done since leaving home or whatever I may do in future, has been and will be done with the sole purpose of bringing about the speedy emancipation of my country and I shall never do anything which will not meet with the approval of nationalist circles in India. Further, I may say that if the cunning, unscrupulous and resourceful British Government has failed to allure or to corrupt me, no power on earth will ever be able to do so. Whatever may happen to me, my one and only duty will be to India and to India alone.

Since coming to Europe I have seen much with my own eyes and I can, therefore, compare the actual conditions here with the lies that

---

[1] Broadcast from Berlin on 1 March 1943, but obviously recorded prior to his departure from Europe on 8 February 1943.

are propagated from the day to day by the B.B.C., that is the 'Bluff and Bluster Corporation' of London. Believe me when I say that Britain is going to lose the war and as a sequel to her crushing defeat the British Empire will be completely dismembered. Whether we actively assist Britain or whether we remain strictly neutral nothing can alter by a hair's breadth the ultimate issue of this titanic struggle. In such a situation it is not only wise and prudent but imperatively necessary for India to play a dynamic role. India must, by her own efforts and her sacrifices, contribute materially to the break-up of the British Empire so that out of the ashes of that empire may emerge a triumphant India which will be the creation of the Indian people.

Friends, it will be an act of political suicide to remain inactive or neutral in this crisis. If we do so we shall either remain enslaved in spite of the dismemberment of the British Empire or we shall receive freedom as a gift from the victorious Tripartite Powers. We want neither. The Indian people must, therefore, fight for and win their liberty. But in this fight some help from abroad will be necessary. I have studied very carefully this struggle for liberty that has gone on all over the world during the last 200 years, but I have not as yet discovered one single instance where freedom was won without outside help of some sort. Where the enemy is a powerful world-empire, the need for outside help is even greater and where that powerful world-empire, namely, Britain, is buttressed by a combination of several other Powers it would be the height of folly not to accept any assistance that may be offered to us. When Britain has been pouring into India war material and soldiers from America, China, Africa and the rest of the British Empire, it does not lie in the mouth of a Britisher to complain if we take help from any other quarter. It will, of course, be for India to decide what help she needs, and the less she needs it, the better it will be for her. We can expect help or assistance only from those who are our friends and allies. In the present case those who are trying to overthrow the British Empire are helping our liberation and are therefore our friends and allies, while all those who are trying to save that empire are only attempting to perpetuate our slavery. But apart from this theoretical proposition, my personal experience as well as my interviews with Herr Hitler and Signor Mussolini have convinced me that in this struggle against British Imperialism, the Tripartite Powers are our best friends and allies outside India.

Friends, I know that my friends like Swami Sahajanad Saraswati may hesitate to believe in the sincerity of the Tripartite Powers. But I would like to remind them that the powers have in their own interest resolved to fight British Imperialism to a finish and they will undoubtedly do so. And the destruction of British power will inevitably help India in throwing off the British yoke. Moreover the whole world, including the Tripartite Powers, would stand to gain if India could liberate herself and the only country to regret India's emancipation would be Britain. In this fateful hour in India's history, it would be a grievous mistake to be carried away by ideological considerations alone. The internal politics of Germany or Italy or Japan do not concern us. They are the concern of the people of those countries. But even a child should understand that whatever the internal politics of the Tripartite Powers may be, their aim in the international sphere is the destruction of the British Empire which is India's one and only enemy. Do we not see with our own eyes how, regardless of ideological considerations, the British Empire is now co-operating with Soviet Russia? It is high time that my friends and colleagues at home learnt to differentiate between the internal and the external policy of free India. The internal policy of free India is and should be the concern of the Indian people themselves, while the external policy should be one of collaboration with the enemies of Britain. While standing for full collaboration with the Tripartite Powers in the external sphere, I stand for absolute self-determination for India where her own national affairs are concerned and I shall never tolerate any interference in the internal affairs of free India. So far as our social and economic problems are concerned, my views are exactly what they were when I was at home, and no one should make the mistake of concluding that external collaboration with the Tripartite Powers means acceptance of their domination or even of their ideology in our internal affairs.

Friends, my task today is to lead the final struggle for India's emancipation. But when that task is fulfilled and India is liberated, it will then be my duty to report to my countrymen and leave it to them to decide what form of government they would like to have. And as I told Mahatma Gandhi in my farewell talk with him in June 1940 before I was taken to prison, I shall again call on him when I have succeeded in my mission to achieve India's liberation from the British yoke. It is a matter of profound joy and pride for all of us that, backed by the full diplomatic support of the Tripartite Powers, our countrymen in the Far East are now assembling in a conference at Bangkok in order to devise ways and means for effecting the speedy emancipation of our motherland. As I have so often said, the last phase of our national struggle began with the departure of Sir Stafford Cripps from India. We shall soon reach a stage when we shall have to take up arms if the Anglo-American forces do not voluntarily vacate India. Friends, prepare for that auspicious day and organise simultaneously for the final battle and to resist the scorched-earth policy by which the British want to wantonly destroy and ruin our country before they fly from India.

The British Empire, today, is in such a tottering condition that I feel convinced that with the right leadership and the necessary assistance, it is possible for the Indian people to achieve their own salvation. This salvation will not be long in coming. In the course of the present war India will win her freedom and I repeat once again that when the hour strikes I shall be at your side ready to participate in the final struggle. The power that could not prevent my getting out of India will not be able to prevent my getting in. Meanwhile, friends, please send a word of cheer to our comrades in prison. Let them patiently bide their time for when they learn of the fighting they will be the first to hail it, and we shall then bring them the arms and equipment which will enable them to be soldiers in India's last war of independence.

Countrymen and friends! Before I proceed any further I want to greet you once again on my behalf and on behalf of all those who are working with me. We would like to tell you first of all that India's brave and courageous fight for liberty has produced a profound impression all over the world. In fact, people did not at first believe the report of British terror and brutality in India, and leaders in England were compelled to make speeches in order to justify large-scale shootings on unarmed men and women in our country. From these speeches the outside world was convinced that India was in a state of rebellion and that the reports emanating from India were quite correct and by no means exaggerated. Friends, I now want to assure you that the news of the internal happenings in India are regularly travelling to all quarters of the globe. The British cannot any longer isolate India from the rest of the world. I have noticed that every day that passes brings to the Indian people more and more sympathy from even the most unexpected quarters. All over the world India is today on the front page of the daily Press; and from the enemies of British Imperialism India can expect not only sympathy but any help that she may need in her struggle for liberty. It is for the Indian people to decide if they need any help from abroad and if so to what extent. Friends, I must also tell you that your countrymen in Europe, America and the Far East fully realise that India has a golden opportunity for overthrowing the British yoke. On the occasion of Independence Day, Indians in Germany expressed their complete solidarity with the struggle now going on at home and they are doing their very best to help and support that struggle. What is more important, many of them have already decided to participate in the last phase of our national struggle.

So far as India is concerned, the next turning point will come soon and when that hour arrives and the last phase of the national struggle begins, India will have to strike her final blow. This last blow, which India will then have to deliver, will be the death blow to the British Empire and it will, therefore, be India's privilege to end that satanic empire. Friends, from what I have myself seen and experienced during my stay abroad, I am convinced more than ever before that the British Empire will be overthrown and broken up and out of the ashes of that empire will emerge a free India. I, therefore, call upon my countrymen to give up fear, doubt and hesitation and come forward to help the national struggle to the best of their ability. Disaster will befall those who still fight with the British Government. It is absolutely clear that time is now working against Britain and her Allies and is working for India. We must, therefore, continue the fight at any cost and by all means. We must definitely make up our minds to continue the fight for at least two years and to sacrifice at least 100,000 lives in the course of the struggle. Long before this period of two years comes to an end India will certainly be free. Our slogan should therefore be: 'We shall fight for two years and we shall sacrifice 100,000 lives for the freedom of our country.' If you can do that and I can do that, I guarantee you success and liberty.

Let me remind you once again that the two-fold object of the non-violent guerilla warfare that you are now carrying on should be: firstly, to paralyse the civil administration in India and secondly, to destroy war production in India. I should also like to tell you that the time has come to intensify our propaganda within the Indian Army. This could be done best by sending our party men in large numbers into the ranks of the Indian Army. In the last phase of the national struggle the Indian Army will have to play an important role.

Friends, you must have realised by now that in future Bengal will have to play a most important role in this fight for freedom. Let all my sisters and brothers in Bengal prepare for this contingency. I must again call upon my sisters and brothers in Ceylon to come forward and march shoulder to shoulder with us for winning our common liberty. This is a golden opportunity not only for India but for Ceylon as well. When India has been waging a gigantic fight for overthrowing the British Imperialism the task of Ceylon has become very much easier than it would otherwise have been. As for India, so also for Ceylon, the watchword should be 'Now or Never.' Ceylon can hope to be free only when she stands and fights with India.

Friends, do not be carried away for one moment by the pretensions and propaganda carried on by Anglo-American agencies. Look at the map of the world yourselves and you will understand the position today. Except in Africa, the Allies have not made any success anywhere in the world worth the name; and even in Africa, the Allies have not achieved what they promised to the whole world. General Eisenhower is still marking time and sometimes retreating in North Africa. To hide the shame of defeat, they have been saying that the most important theatre of war is Russia and not Africa. In Europe, British power and influence simply does not exist. In Russia, the real position will be apparent to anybody who looks at the respective positions of the two armies. In the Far East, the Anglo-Americans have received a shattering defeat and Japanese forces now stand on the eastern frontiers of India. The repeated declarations of the Japanese Prime Minister, General Tojo, have informed the world and the Indian people as to what the Japanese policy in Asia is and what Japanese policy towards India really is. The final decision of this war will be not in Africa but in Europe and in Asia; and one can see for himself where the Anglo-American forces stand today in Europe and in Asia. They are in a desperate position, and any amount of loud and boastful propaganda cannot save them.

Friends, in conclusion, I call upon you to exert yourself to the utmost in this most critical hour in our history. Victory is assured. Time is working for us. Our Allies abroad are all ready to help us. What more can we desire? We have only to continue the struggle, come what may and no matter what the sacrifice may be. Be confident that India is going to be free and that before long.

Down with British Imperialism! Long Live Free India! Long Live Revolution!

38

The 24th Anniversary of the Bloodbath of Amritsar

SPEECH, END JANUARY/EARLY FEBRUARY 1943[1]

Countrymen and friends!

Events have passed rapidly since I addressed you on the Jallianwallah Bagh Day last year. Empires have crashed in East Asia and the face of India has completely changed. The liberation of Burma from the British yoke has given a new encouragement to India in her fight against British Imperialism. The myth of British invincibility has been smashed and the self-confidence of the peoples under British rule from Egypt right up to India has received an added vigour. The last illusions about the sincerity of British democratic professions having been shattered, the Indian National Congress gave the impetus to a civil disobedience campaign. This campaign, described by Mahatma Gandhi as an open rebellion, has been giving sleepless nights to the British Government for the last eight months. This campaign has attained such dimensions that the alien government have thought it fit to let loose a wave of terror on India. But the conflagration has spread so wide that the most ruthless and barbaric measures applied by the British oppressor have failed to extinguish the flames. Machine gunning, aerial bombardment, tear gas, bayonet charges, capital punishment—none of the these ruthless measures have succeeded in cowing down the unarmed masses of Indians.

Incidents like the Amritsar Massacre have taken place so frequently during the last eight months that today that incident of 24 years ago

---

[1] Read in absentia in Hotel Kaiserhof and broadcast over Azad Hind Radio on 13 April 1943, and printed in *Azad Hind* (3/4, 1943), but obviously recorded prior to his departure from Europe on 8 February 1943.

does no longer represent the only one of its kind staged by the British on the soil of India.

Yet, the Amritsar Massacre remains a symbol of the freedom, peace and order given by the British to India. This bloody incident exposed all the hypocrisy of British Democracy; Britain pretended to fight the last war for the freedom of nations, for the right of self-determination of peoples and for making the world safe for Democracy. India, believing in the high-sounding professions of Britain and in the categorical promise of freedom given to her played an active role in war. At the end of the war, India expected at least a Dominion Status; but she got bullets instead. The cold-blooded massacre of thousands of men, women and children gathered in the Jalianwalla Bagh, was the brutal reply of Britain to a peaceful demand of primary human rights. This incident shook the faith of India in Britain. It gave the impulse to a revolutionary movement, which would no longer trust in the sham Democracy of Britain. India was determined never again to fall in the trap laid by her oppressor and never again to commit the same blunder as in the Great War.

It was small wonder, therefore, that when the present war broke out, Indian nationalists took an extremely critical attitude towards the words and deeds of Britain. The Forward Bloc openly advocated the idea that the enemies of Britain were the natural allies of India. England's difficulty was India's only opportunity and we were determined to make the best of it. The Congress refused to accept the delusive proposals brought by Sir Stafford Cripps. And all attempts at a peaceful settlement having failed, the present campaign was launched. This campaign, which will also be our last struggle for independence, differs in many respects with the civil disobedience movements of the last 23 years. The present struggle shows some unique characteristics, which are the best guarantee of our final victory. Firstly, the people of India, irrespective of class and creed, are united as never before in this struggle against British Imperialism. Secondly, the British have completely failed in their efforts to channelise the struggle into communal riots. Thirdly, the movement has not been confined to the so-called British India. It has spread also to the Indian States. Fourthly, the confidence of the people in their final victory is absolute and unshakable. Fifthly, the movement is not limited to non-violence. The people are using violence and weapons wherever possible and necessary.

Countrymen and Friends at home! I take this opportunity to congratulate you on the heroism and persistency that you have shown in the fight against British imperialism. Your attitude has won for you the respect and sympathy of the world. The happenings in India have exposed British hypocrisy to the World; and no serious-minded person believes today either in the anti-Indian propaganda of Britain or in her high professions. This fact in itself is encouraging enough. Besides this, there are two factors of vital importance which should strengthen your confidence in your final victory. Firstly, the British Empire is crumbling down to pieces and no force on earth will be able to save it from its final doom. Secondly, India does not stand alone in her fight against Britain. The Tripartite Powers are as much interested in the destruction of the British Empire, as is India. Our strategy must be to make the best use of this situation. We must do our part to hasten the destruction of British power in India, the very heart of the Empire. Once it ceases to beat, the Empire will exist no more. If you find at a certain stage that your best efforts are no longer enough to bring about the collapse of British power, you are free to ask as much help as you find necessary from the Tripartite Powers. But you must accept the main task of systematically harassing and exhausting the enemy. Because, if we would deserve freedom, we must fight for it. Freedom that may come as a gift from the victorious powers we shall never be able to keep. The blood of the martyr is the price that must be paid for liberty. As I have been telling you, we must be ready to undergo all sorts of suffering and sacrifices during this last struggle of Indian independence. As I have stated on several other occasions, you must be prepared to sacrifice at least one hundred thousand lives on the altar of liberty. And you must conserve energies to last for a struggle of two years' duration. Your countrymen and comrades abroad are doing all that is humanly possible to bring you help in right time. It would be foolish to imagine that the British Government would capitulate without the force of arms. An armed struggle must necessarily follow the present campaign. Your countrymen abroad are preparing for this armed struggle, which will deliver a deathblow to British power in India. I assure you that when the proper moment arrives we shall be fighting shoulder to shoulder with you against our brutal oppressor. In the meanwhile, your struggle must go on with an unflinching belief in the justness of our course, and without the slightest thought of a compromise with our century-old oppressor whose main virtues are hypocrisy and falsehood, greed and ruthlessness. The present fight is an indispensable preliminary to the final armed struggle. And the success of the latter will much depend on the thoroughness with which the former is carried out. The immediate objectives of the present fight are: firstly, to paralyse the civil administration, and secondly, to bring war production to a standstill. The better you can accomplish this task, the nearer will be your victory.

Sisters and Brothers!

As I told you at the beginning of this year, the future course of this war will be decided in the current year. And the decision of this war will fall in Europe and Asia. Despite British propaganda, time is working definitely against England, and in favour of her enemies. The Anglo-Americans have so far failed to erect a second front in Europe. The offensive of Marshall Wavell for the resubjugation of Burma has proved a complete failure. The Tripartite powers are day by day consolidating their strength for the final blow against the Anglo-Americans. In the scheme of Anglo-American strategy India occupies such a vital position that a great responsibility in destruction of British Imperialism must rest on her shoulders. If we realise this responsibility, victory will undoubtedly be ours. And in the new order that will come India will fulfil her destined role of a veritable link assuring the friendship and understanding between East and West. The free India that will emerge out of the ashes of the British Empire will reassume her mission of contributing to the peace, happiness and progress of humanity.

Countrymen at home and abroad!

In the sacred memory of the martyrs of Amritsar let us today swear the destruction of British Power in India. Let us today refresh our memories of British terrorism and breach of good faith. Let us to day swear our oath to do or die for the complete independence of India.

The 13th of April has been observed as a day of national mourning all over India for the last 23 years. I am confident that soon the time will come when this day will be celebrated as India's national festival of emancipation and victory.

39

On the Path of Danger

LETTER TO SARAT CHANDRA BOSE,
8 FEBRUARY 1943[1]

My dear brother,

Today once again I am embarking on the path of danger. But this time towards home. I may not see the end of the road. If I meet with any such danger, I will not be able to send you any further news in this life. That is why today I am leaving my news here—it will reach you in due time. I have married here and I have a daughter. In my absence please show my wife and daughter the love that you have given me throughout your life. May my wife and daughter complete and successfully fulfill my unfinished tasks—that is my ultimate prayer.

Please accept my *pronam* and convey the same to Mother, Mejobowdidi[2] and other elders.

Berlin, 8 February 1943   Your devoted brother,

SUBHAS

---

[1] Translated from the original Bengali.
  Just before starting on his perilous submarine journey from Europe to Asia Subhas Chandra Bose wrote this letter to his elder brother Sarat Chandra Bose in his own hand in Bengali. After this letter reached Sarat Chandra Bose, he visited Vienna in 1948 with his wife Bivabati and three of his children—Sisir, Roma and Chitra—and warmly welcomed Emilie and Anita into the Bose family.

[2] Sarat Chandra Bose's wife, Bivabati.